INDEX

The missed Putsch

History of Coups

Turkey plunged into chaos on 15/7/2016 as forces loyal to President Recep Tayyip Erdogan quashed a coup attempt in a night of explosions, air battles and gunfire that left scores dead. Thousands were arrested amid vows the plotters would "pay a heavy price for their treason."

The military staged three coups between 1960 and 1980 and pressured Prime Minister Necmettin Erbakan, a pious Muslim mentor of Erdogan who was disliked by Turkey's secular establishment, out of power in 1997. In 2007, the military threatened to intervene in a presidential election and warned the government to curb Islamic influences, but the action backfired and Abdullah Gul, the candidate favored by a government with Islamic leanings, took office.

The latest coup attempt surprised observers because Erdogan's government had taken steps to bring the military to heel, including dismissals and prosecutions of high-ranking active and former officers for alleged coup plots. Erdogan's government appeared to be working effectively with the military, coordinating on national security issues and confronting a perceived anti-government faction said to have infiltrated the police and other institutions.

The Turkish military has traditionally seen itself as the guardian of Turkey's old secular establishment, a legacy of national founder and former army officer Mustafa Kemal Ataturk, as well as an enforcer of order in times of civil unrest and weak civilian leadership. While it was forced to lower its political profile under Erdogan's government, Turkey's military has been buffeted by a renewed conflict with Kurdish separatist rebels and bombings by suspected Islamic extremists, including an attack on Istanbul's main airport that killed dozens. Erdogan has also been a polarizing leader, though he commands deep support among a pious Muslim class that once felt marginalized under past military-influenced governments.

Turkey is a NATO member and a key partner in US-led efforts to defeat the Islamic State group, which controls territory in Syria and Iraq, and has allowed American fighter jets to use its Incirlik air base to fly missions against the extremists. Turkey's strategic location in the Mideast region, straddling the

Asian and European continents, makes it a critical player in international conflicts. In 2003, Turkey barred US forces from using its territory in the invasion of Iraq, raising questions about whether the politically powerful Turkish military had undercut a civilian-led initiative to help the Americans.

Timeline of the "coup"

15/7/2016

10 p.m. - Shots are heard inside the General Staff headquarters in Ankara and a helicopter fires at people on the ground. Soldiers take control of state broadcaster TRT and the General Staff headquarters in Ankara as troops and tanks block the Bosphorus and Fatih Sultan Mehmet bridges linking Asia and Europe in Istanbul

11:24 p.m. - An explosion is heard at the police special operations center in Gölbaşı, south of Ankara.

11:30 p.m. - Prime Minister Binali Yıldırım announces an "attempt to stage a coup" was happening during a live TV broadcast.

11:30 p.m. - Chief of General Staff Gen. Hulusi Akar is taken hostage by pro-coup soldiers.

12:05 a.m. - Security sources tell Anadolu Agency the coup attempt was being staged by officers with alleged links to U.S.-based Islamic scholar Fethullah Gülen, who is accused of leading a terrorist organization.

12:11 a.m. - President Recep Tayyip Erdoğan leaves Marmaris, in Turkey's southwest, for Atatürk International Airport in Istanbul.

12:13 a.m. - A TRT news anchor is forced to read a declaration from coup leaders, who had named themselves the "Peace at Home Committee," claiming to have taken control of the country. Erdoğan later addresses the country on CNN Türk via a mobile telephone, urging people to "take to the streets" to resist the coup and defend democracy.

12:35 a.m. - The first investigation into the coup is launched by a prosecutor in Istanbul.

1 a.m. - The Ankara police headquarters is attacked by jets and helicopters.

1:39 a.m. - The first arrests of pro-coup soldiers are made.

2:20 a.m. - The Gölbaşı Police Special Forces Department headquarters is bombed by a pro-coup aircraft, killing 17 police officers and two personnel from satellite operator Turksat.

2:30 a.m. – A total of 13 soldiers, including three senior officers, are held while attempting to enter the Presidential Palace in Ankara. A spokesman for the National Intelligence Agency (MİT) says the coup has been "thwarted."

2:42 a.m. – 2:49 a.m. - The Turkish parliament is targeted by jets and helicopters. More than 10 are injured in the bombing.

3 a.m. - TRT resumes broadcasting.

3:20 a.m. - Erdoğan lands in Istanbul.

3:23 a.m. – A military helicopter carrying two captains and 12 soldiers lands in the parking lot of the Doğan Media Center in Istanbul and enters the daily Hürriyet building adjacent to the Doğan TV Center. Soldiers forcefully take everyone out and intervene in CNN Türk broadcasts.

7:35 a.m. - More than 750 military personnel are held over coup allegations.

8:32 a.m. - Gen. Akar is rescued from pro-coup forces.

9:40 a.m. - 200 soldiers surrender to police in Ankara.

9:46 a.m. - Treason charges are laid against retired Air Force Commander Gen. Akın Öztürk and Lt. Gen. Metin İyidil, commander of the Land Forces Training and Doctrine Command.

9:58 a.m. - Judicial recess is cancelled.

10:37 a.m. - Yıldırım announces that Gen. Akar is back on-duty.

11:27 a.m. - Coup forces at General Staff headquarters ask to negotiate surrender. Three prosecutors later receive the surrender of the troops.

12:57 p.m. - Yıldırım announces that 161 people had been killed and 1,440 had been injured during the coup attempt and more than 2,800 military personnel involved in the "vile attempt" had been arrested.

2:37 p.m. - 2,745 judges are suspended over alleged links to the coup attempt. A detention order is issued for all of them later in the day.

5:00 p.m. – The Turkish parliament holds an extraordinary session, where ruling and opposition party leaders address lawmakers. A joint anti-coup declaration signed by all four parties in parliament is read out.

8:02 p.m. - An operation at Akıncı Air Base northwest of Ankara, which had served as the coup headquarters and where the top generals were held hostage, ends.

Background

A group calling itself the *"Council for Peace in the Homeland"* declared martial law and a curfew late Friday 15/7/2016, saying it had launched the coup *"to ensure and restore constitutional order, democracy, human rights and freedoms and let the supremacy of the law in the country prevail…"*.

No named military officer claimed responsibility for the actions. Erdogan put the blame for the coup on supporters of his arch-foe, US-based Turkish cleric Fethullah Gulen, whose Hizmet movement has a powerful presence in Turkish society, including the media, police and judiciary. Gulen denied being behind the coup attempt and condemned it *"in the strongest terms."* Government-backed jets downed pro-coup aircraft and bombed tanks surrounding the presidential palace in the capital Ankara. Turkish security officers detain Turkish police officers (in black) on July 15, 2016 in Istanbul, during a security shutdown of the Bosphorus Bridge. Turkish security officers detain Turkish police officers (in black) on July 15, 2016 in Istanbul, during a security shutdown of the Bosphorus Bridge. Dozens of soldiers backing the coup surrendered on the Bosphorus bridge in Istanbul they had held throughout the night, holding their hands above their heads as they were detained.

Nearly 200 soldiers surrendered at the military headquarters in Ankara on Saturday, 16/7/2016. An official said special forces were currently securing the complex. Istanbul authorities sought to make a show of normalization with the bridges reopening to traffic and Ataturk International Airport — which had been shut down by the plotters — gradually reopening.

But Erdogan, who had called on people during the night to take to the streets to help foil the coup, urged them in a late morning Twitter message to stay out *"because a new flare-up could take place at any moment."* Turkish Prime Minister Binali Yildirim said in Ankara on Saturday *"the situation is completely under control."* He was flanked by the ministers of justice and interior as well as Turkey's top general outside his offices in the capital.

The acting army chief, General Umit Dundar, said earlier that the coup attempt had been foiled. Authorities had regained control of the parliament, which was hastily reconvened into a session broadcast live on television. A total of 2,839 soldiers had been arrested, Yildirim said. Erdogan flew back to Istanbul in the early hours of Saturday, saying the hotel he was staying at on Turkey's Aegean coast was bombed after he left.

Erdogan appointed Dundar, commander of the First Army, as acting chief of staff after General Hulusi Akar was captured by putschists. Akar was later rescued, the private TV station CNN-Turk reported. More than 250 people have been killed overall. Yildirim said Saturday 161 people had been killed and that 1,440 had been wounded, while acting army chief General Umit Dundar said 104 coup plotters were dead.

Erdogan had called his supporters out onto the streets, and in several locations they outnumbered putsch soldiers. A civilian killed by Turkish soldiers lies on the ground on the Bosphorus bridge in Istanbul on July 16, 2016, following an attempt by discontented soldiers to seize power from President Recep Tayyip Erdogan that claimed more than 250 lives. A civilian killed by Turkish soldiers lies on the ground on the Bosphorus bridge in Istanbul on July 16, 2016, following a deadly attempted military coup.

Putsch troops had moved to block the bridges across the Bosphorus Strait in Istanbul, and an photographer saw soldiers open fire on people gathered near one of them, leaving dozens wounded. Soldiers also shot at protesters angrily denouncing the coup bid at Istanbul's famous Taksim Square, injuring several. Explosions rocked areas near official buildings as government aircraft sought to eject pro-coup tanks.

Turkish media on Saturday named former Turkish Air Force chief Akın Ozturk as one of the main instigators of the country's attempted coup on Friday. Ozturk, who led the air force between 2013 and 2015 before retiring from the army last year, was also the nation's military attaché to Israel in the 1990s; he served in the Jewish state between 1996-1998.

Gulen has harshly condemned the attempted coup attempt by military officers that resulted in a night of explosions, air battles and gunfire that left dozens dead. But Turkish President Recep Tayyip Erdogan's government is blaming the chaos on the cleric, who lives in exile in Pennsylvania and promotes a philosophy that blends a mystical form of Islam with staunch advocacy of democracy, education, science and interfaith dialogue.

Erdogan has long accused Gulen, a former ally, of trying to overthrow the government. Washington has never found any evidence particularly compelling previously. Gulen is understood to maintain significant support among some members of the military and mid-level bureaucrats. His movement called Hizmet includes think tanks, schools and various media enterprises. Gulen and Erdogan only became estranged in recent years.

In a statement, Gulen said he condemned, *"in the strongest terms, the attempted military coup in Turkey."* *"Government should be won through a process of free and fair elections, not force,"* he said. *"I pray to God for Turkey, for Turkish citizens, and for all those currently in Turkey that this situation is resolved peacefully and quickly."*

Gulen sharply rejected any responsibility: *"As someone who suffered under multiple military coups during the past five decades, it is especially insulting to be accused of having any link to such an attempt. I categorically deny such accusations.*

President Tayyip Erdoğan, Prime Minister Binali Yıldırım and many politicians from different parties were pretty quick to say that Fethullah Gülen, the Islamist ideologue living in the U.S., was the mastermind of the failed coup attack. The government calls Gülen members in the state the *"parallel structure organization within the state."* The military sources, who are among the majority who stood against the junta, claim that some of them were known or suspected sympathizers of Gülen. Reliable sources say *"don't bet on the probability that he is not involved,"* despite the fact that no direct link has been proven so far (though it is early), and despite Gülen denying the accusations.

There are a few scenarios that are not very convincing. But the one about the Supreme Military Council's (YAŞ) meetings about retirements and promotions, expected to take place at the end of July, might have a point. Reliable sources claimed that after understanding there would be a purge against "parallel state" members within the Turkish Armed Forces (TSK), followers of Gülen decided to make this move as a "last chance" to take the state apparatus under control.

This possibility is now being looked into by both government inspectors and the in-house inspection of the military. There is a suspicion that some officers were approached by the group to take part and agreed out of their dislike of Erdoğan. The image of the military as the most trusted institution in Turkey, acting within its disciplined chain of command as the guardian of the country and the republic, did not stand up this time. It is understood that there was a well and secretly organized group with political aims that reached into the upper echelons of the military, as well as penetrating the lower levels.

The fact that his private secretary, a colonel who took Chief of General Staff Gen. Hulusi Akar hostage, and the body guards of Air Force commander Abidin Ünal, who kidnapped him on behalf of the plotters, are traumatic for the military, the government and the people. The military is likely to now undergo under a significant restructuring after the failed coup plot.

It is not likely to affect Turkey's foreign policy as long as NATO commitments are fulfilled, but it may negatively affect the country's security situation. There are reports that some important Turkish anti-terrorism experts were killed by the plotters in their raid on the Police Special Forces facilities in Gölbaşı near Ankara, as well as elsewhere. That might also affect Turkey's struggle against the outlawed Kurdistan Workers' Party (PKK) and the Islamic State of Iraq and the Levant (ISIL).

There was also an attack on the National Intelligence Agency (MİT) headquarters, though there have been no reports of causalities there yet. Among those detained are 2nd Army Commander Gen. Adem Huduti, who was in charge of security along the Syria and Iraq borders, Lt. Gen. Erdal Özturk of the 3rd Corps in Istanbul, which is also the NATO contingency force, and the commander of the strategic İncirlik Air Base used in the fight against ISIL in Syria by the U.S.-led coalition.

Deputy Foreign Minister Numan Kurtulmuş said on CNN Türk on July 17 that they had heard nothing about such an organization in advance and, had they known, they could have taken precautions. That also puts both the police force under the Interior Ministry and the MİT face-to-face with hard questions, as well as the military's own counter-intelligence. One of Erdoğan's closest aides, his PR and election campaign advisor Erol Olçak, and his 16-year-old son were killed in the front line of protesters. What's more, Erdoğan certainly would not like to see his authority, especially in the military where he is proud of being the commander-in-chief, denied.

Crackdown

A crackdown on the military and the judiciary in the wake of a failed coup attempt has led to the detention of thousands of soldiers and judges and prosecutors, including commanders and top court members. Justice Minister Bekir Bozdağ on July 17 said around 6,000 suspects, including at least 2,839 soldiers and thousands of judiciary members, have been detained as part of a wide-scale operation launched following the deadly coup attempt initiated by a group of soldiers late on July 15.

"There are currently around 6,000 detentions. It will surpass 6,000. The legal process on these will continue," said Bozdağ. Suspects are being charged with *"membership of an armed terrorist organization"* and *"attempting to overthrow the government of the Turkish Republic using force and violence or attempting to completely or partially hinder its function."*

The Ankara Governor's Office also announced on July 17 that 149 police personnel were suspended from their duties for having links to the coup attempt. The terrorist organization is allegedly led by the U.S.-based Islamic scholar Fethullah Gülen, a friend turned foe of the Turkish government.

The arrest warrants target two members of the Constitutional Court, Alparslan Altan and Erdal Tercan, 48 members of the Council of State, and 140 members of the Supreme Court of Appeals. The detention of 2,745 judicial and administrative judges and prosecutors was ordered after they were suspended from duty by the Supreme Council of Judges and Prosecutors (HSYK) early on June 16.

Many commanders have also been detained and some of them were later arrested. Among the most significant names detained was the chief military assistant to Turkish President Recep Tayyip Erdoğan, Col. Ali Yazıcı; the commander of the 2nd Army, Gen. Adem Huduti; the executive officer and Malatya Garrison Commander Avni Angun; and the commander of the 3rd Army, Gen. Erdal Öztürk.

Air Forces Commander Akın Öztürk was also detained on suspicion of masterminding the coup attempt, according to multiple reports. In addition, Adana İncirlik 10th Adana Tanker Base Commander Gen. Bekir Ercan was among those detained.

The jets that hit Ankara were reportedly supported by Turkish tanker aircrafts based at the İncirlik Air Base, which is also being used by the U.S.-led coalition in the fight against the Islamic State of Iraq and the Levant (ISIL). Police also detained eight Air Force generals suspected of being appointed to the top "coup command posts" if the failed attempt had succeeded, at Istanbul's Sabiha Gökçen Airport late on July 16.

In the Aegean province of İzmir, Aegean Army Deputy Commander Brig. Mamduh Hakbilken and Foça Marine Amphibious Force Brigadier Commander Commodore Halil İbrahim Yıldız were among those detained. Meanwhile operations in Turkey's eastern and southeastern provinces also took place, with Brig. Arif Seddar Afşar in Bitlis, Brig. Yunus Kotaman in Bingöl, Brig. Abdülkerim Ünlü in Tunceli, Brig. Ahmet Şimşek in Siirt, and Maj. Gen. Halil İbrahim Ergin in Hakkari all being detained.

On July 17, meanwhile, an operation was carried out on the Istanbul Gendarmerie Commandership, with police searching Istanbul Provincial Gendarmerie Commander Staff Col. Gürcan Sercan's office. Several other provincial gendarmerie commanders were also detained as part of the operations throughout Turkey.

Eight generals, namely Brig. İrfan Can, Maj. Gen. İmdat Bahri Biber, Maj. Gen. Fethi Alpay, Maj. Gen. Haluk Sahar, Maj. Gen. Mehmet Özlü, Brig. Ahmet Biçer, Maj. Gen. Şaban Umut and Maj. Gen. Serdar Gülbaş were detained. Meanwhile, the general assembly of the HSYK decided to end the membership of five of its judges who were facing detention demands from the Ankara Chief Prosecutor's Office, while it also cut short the vacations of some other judges and prosecutors.

The Bakırköy Prosecutor's Office in Istanbul ordered the detention, in line with the HSYK's demand, of some 140 judges and prosecutors on duty at the Bakırköy, Küçükçekmece and district administrative courts early on July 17. At least 290 people were killed and thousands of others were wounded in the coup attempt. People took to the streets throughout Turkey on the evening of July 15 with shots being heard inside the General Staff headquarters in Ankara and a helicopter firing at people on the ground.

While a group of soldiers then took control of state broadcaster TRT and the General Staff headquarters in Ankara, troops and tanks blocked the Bosphorus and Fatih Sultan Mehmet bridges linking Asia and Europe in Istanbul. An explosion was heard at the police special operations center in Gölbaşı, south of Ankara, shortly after Yıldırım announced that an "attempt to stage a coup" was happening during a live TV broadcast.

Chief of General Staff Gen. Hulusi Akar was held hostage by pro-coup soldiers until he was rescued on June 16. The coup attempt was confirmed nation-wide when the TRT building was raided by a group of soldiers and a news anchor was forced to read a declaration from the coup leaders, who had named themselves the "Peace at Home Committee," claiming to have taken control of the country.

President Recep Tayyip Erdoğan later addressed the country on CNN Türk via a mobile telephone, urging people to "take to the streets" to resist the coup and defend democracy. After the president's call thousands of people headed to Istanbul's bridges and Atatürk Airport, as well as Taksim Square, to stage demonstrations against the coup attempt. There were major incidents in which crowds of civilians and police officers had violent encounters with pro-coup soldiers.

As protesters poured onto the streets, troops opened fire on people gathered near one of the bridges, killing five. Soldiers also shot at protesters angrily denouncing the coup bid at Istanbul's iconic Taksim Square, injuring several. While the first investigation into the coup was launched by a prosecutor in Istanbul, the Ankara police headquarters was attacked by jets and helicopters and the Gölbaşı police special forces department headquarters was bombed by a pro-coup aircraft, killing 17 police officers and two personnel from satellite operator Turksat.

The events were followed by a total of 13 soldiers, including three senior officers, being held while attempting to enter the Presidential Palace in Ankara. Shortly after, the Turkish parliament was targeted by jets and helicopters in an attack by the pro-coup soldiers and more than 10 are injured in the bombing. The coup operations of the soldiers had begun to reach an end when some of its forces at the General Staff headquarters asked to negotiate surrender. Three prosecutors later received the surrender of the troops, while a series of other forces also surrendered.

In its first statement following the coup attempt, the Turkish Armed Forces yesterday praised the role of the Turkish people in stopping the plotters, underlining that it will continue to be *"at the service of the state and the people."* *"The biggest role in preventing this treacherous act belongs to our honorable people. These plotters belonging to the illegal structure have been stopped and will be given the heaviest penalty,"* the military said in a written statement.

It said a majority of the army and the police department firmly stood against the coup plotters, which meant the attempt could be neutralized before accomplishing its aim. It also noted that many members of the public took to the streets to protect *"the real members of the Turkish Armed Forces"* and to foil the coup, which it said would have dealt a serious blow to Turkey's democracy.

The crackdown on alleged coup plotters has spread to the country's police department, with a total of 7,850 police officers, including high-ranking officials, suspended on the night of July 17. A list of the suspended personnel was sent to the provincial chiefs by Police Chief Mehmet Celalettin Lekesiz. The suspended police officers were called to the provincial police headquarters throughout the night and their weapons and police IDs were confiscated.

The operation within the police came in the wake of a failed coup attempt that started late July 15 and was crushed on June 16. At least 290 people, including more than 100 coup supporters, were killed during the attempt. More than 6,000 suspects in the military and the judiciary, including top commanders and supreme court judges, have been detained in the wake of the failed coup attempt.

This is not the first time Turkey police witness huge suspensions. The last couple of years saw various such actions against the members of the *"parallel state,"* alleged followers of Fethullah Gülen, an Islamic scholar in self-exile in the U.S. whose followers are also accused of being the mastermind of the failed July 15 coup attempt.

Personal stories

A number of personal stories have begun to emerge following the failed coup attempt in Turkey on July 15, which largely took place in the capital Ankara and the country's biggest city, Istanbul. Turgut Aslan, a department head of the Security General Directorate's anti-terror unit, was found shot in the head on July 16 after he had been held hostage by coup plotters. Soldiers had summoned Arslan to the Gendarmerie General Command in Ankara, saying there was an urgent meeting.

Special operations police officers conducted a seven-hour-long operation on the command building, killing 16 coup plotters and capturing another 250 inside. Aslan, who was heavily wounded, was transferred to hospital. In addition, a number of people protested against the coup on Istanbul's Bosphorus Bridge in the early hours of the attempt as soldiers blocked traffic. Thousands of people arrived at the bridge after a call from officials to take to the streets. Soldiers then began to open fire on civilians. Erol Olçok, who was the owner of an advertising agency, and his son, Abdullah Olçok, were killed in the fire.

Meanwhile, Istanbul Security General Directorate head Mustafa Çalışkan also went to the bridge in an effort to prevent the coup attempt. Soldiers opened fire on Çalışkan and his two bodyguards. Münir Alkan, one of the bodyguards, was killed in the fire while Çalışkan escaped unharmed. Police officer Mehmet Önay was also wounded in the fire. Soldiers on the bridge subsequently surrendered to security forces at around 6:30 a.m.

However, a group of people with belts and sharp objects ran towards the soldiers on the bridge, reportedly lynching six of them. Some of the wounded soldiers were struck with iron bars while others were dragged on the ground. The crowd tried to throw the lifeless bodies of soldiers from the bridge but faced police intervention. One soldier was allegedly decapitated during the incidents on the bridge.

Many people standing in front of tanks in the streets in Istanbul and Ankara also prevented the coup attempt, as police detained hundreds of soldiers during operations. Tanks rolled over cars parked on the roads to prevent them from driving toward security buildings.

In Istanbul, some also tried to lynch soldiers blocking the road in the city's Göztepe neighborhood. One captain shot himself in the stomach, while police units later stopped the soldiers from being lynched. Student soldiers in Istanbul's Kuleli Military High School were also reportedly taken to streets by their commanders, who claimed it was for a drill. They seized weapons of police officers in the Çengelköy police station. An armed conflict erupted and 10 people were killed. Special operations police officers later raided the school and detained many students.

In addition, soldiers at Istanbul's Atatürk Airport said in their initial testimonies that they thought they were on a drill but later realized it was a coup when people climbed onto their tanks. Col. Mustafa Kol, the commander of the coup attempt at the airport, tried to enter the principal room but faced a police officer who drew his gun and said, "I will shoot if you come here." Kol later withdrew and police detained soldiers with the help of the crowd which had gathered outside the airport.

Political Islam

Erbakan and Milli Gurus

Beginning in the 1950s and peaking in the 1980s, a number of developments greatly advanced Turkey's modernization. These same events also transformed Turkish politics. The result was a confrontation between provincial/traditional and urban/modern cultures, new social classes, and the fragmentation of the conservative electorate from the 1970s onward. This same situation provided the environment for the growth of Islamist parties in Turkey taking votes away from their center-right competitors.

Islamist political movements vary greatly among different states in their doctrines and strategies. Turkey's groups have their own distinctive history. In Turkey, the Islamist movement emerged soon after the founding of the secular republic in 1923. It was led by tarikat (religious order) sheikhs and professional men of religion, who lost their status and economic power when secular reforms abolished religious institutions. Trying to stage revolts against the secular state in the 1920s and 1930s, it failed to gain wide support and was crushed by the authorities. In general, though, Islamist groups stayed underground during the era of one-party rule, between 1923 and 1946.

With the transition to a multi-party system in 1946, Islamist groups formed covert and overt alliances with the ruling center-right Democratic Party (1950-1960). After the Democratic Party won the 1950 elections, it softened secularist policies. With the provision of civil liberties by the 1961 constitution, Islamist groups began to operate legally (though their activities were still technically banned). Until Necmettin Erbakan established the National Order Party (NOP), the predecessor of the three succeeding Islamist parties, in January 1970, Islamists had either formed conservative factions in a center-right party or had remained underground. With the NOP, however, the Islamists for the first time had an autonomous party organization through which they could campaign for their agenda. Since the NOP's founding, the same Islamist party has endured, albeit under different names: NOP (1970-1971), NSP (1972-1981), Welfare (1983-1998), Virtue (1997-2001)

The NOP largely represented Anatolian cities controlled by religiously conservative Sunnis, and the small traders and artisans (esnaf) of the hinterland. These groups had long waited to benefit from the state's modernization policies but had rarely done so, partly due to their own resistance to modernization in the name of religion and tradition (e.g., female children were not often sent to school). In addition to the frustrated periphery, the NOP also represented religiously conservative people who were informal members of outlawed religious orders. These people formed silent but powerful pressure groups with a large network.

The NOP was shut down by the Constitutional Court on May 20, 1971-after military pressure-on the grounds that it violated the principles of laicism laid down in the Constitution (the preample and Articles 2,19,57) and in the Law of Political Parties (Law No. 648 Articles 92, 93,94). As a result, the National Salvation Party (NSP) was founded in October 1972 to succeed the NOP. With support from provincial merchants, the esnaf, and the covert network of two leading, informally-organized religious groups, the Nakshibandis and Nurcus, the NSP achieved a surprising electoral success in the 1973 general elections, obtaining 11.8 percent of the total vote, mainly in central and eastern Anatolia.

After its solid showing in the 1973 general elections, the NSP became a coalition partner in successive governments. First, it formed a government with the staunchly secularist People's Republican Party (CHP), led by Bulent Ecevit. Soon after, it managed to place its members in the bureaucracy, particularly the ministries that it controlled. Moreover, it succeeded in passing a bill that made theological high schools (imam-hatip) equal to secondary schools and enabled these school's often pro-Islamist students to attend universities. A large number of girls also enrolled in these schools. Many graduates have gone on to political power as Islamists in the 1980s and 1990s (e.g., the mayor of Istanbul, Recep Tayip Erdogan), and have formed a powerful pressure group.

Ecevit's coalition government collapsed following Turkey's July 1974 military operation in Cyprus to protect the Turkish-Cypriot community. The NSP then became a coalition partner in a new "National Front" government on March 31, 1975, formed under the premiership of the center-right Justice Party (JP), led by Suleyman Demirel. This coalition also included the ultra-nationalist National Action Party (NAP) led by Alpaslan Turkes.

In the June 1977 general elections, the NSP suffered a setback, winning only 8.6 percent of the vote, but was included in the second National Front Government formed by Demirel after the elections.

In July 1977 Demirel resigned, but returned to power in August, at the head of an almost identical coalition including the NSP, NAP and JP. However, Demirel was forced to resign again following defections from the JP in December. Ecevit formed a coalition government in January 1978, promising to deal with the economic problems and political violence that were increasing as a result of the clashes between left-right clashes as well as between Sunnis and Alevis. But JP's victory at by-elections in October 1979 deprived Ecevit of his working majority, and he resigned. In November 1979, Demirel formed an all-JP minority government with the backing of the NAP and NSP. In short, the NSP had quickly grown to become a regular member of government coalitions.

In the late 1970s, successive governments failed to solve the country's serious economic and political problems as antagonism between the radical left and radical right escalated into violent clashes bordering on civil war. The armed forces, led by General Kenan Evren, seized power in a bloodless coup and restructured the political system with a new military-drafted constitution in 1982. The leading parties, including the JP, NAP, and NSP, were banned from political activity.

On July 19, 1983 the Welfare Party (RP) was formed under the leadership of Ali Turkmen, in place of the banned Erbakan, replacing the NSP. However, Erbekan was eventually reinstated into Turkish politics and became the Welfare Party's leader. In the first general elections entered under Erbakan's leadership, in November 1987, RP received 7.2 percent of the total vote. In the 1989 local elections it polled 9.8 percent, showing signs of increased support in Istanbul and capturing municipalities in several districts. In the October 1991 general elections, RP formed an electoral alliance with the ultra-nationalist party of Turkes and together obtained 16.7 percent of the total vote. During this time the Islamist movement drew the support of larger segments of the population, the majority of which were moving from rural to urban centers.

One important strategy used by the Islamist movement was to develop an educated counter-elite as a base of support, especially by strengthening the Islamic stream in the educational system. During the post-1980 coup period, governments perceived Islamic education in the schools as a panacea against extremist ideologies.

As Islamist supporters moved from provincial towns and villages to urban centers, they were more likely to gain access to formal education and opportunities for upward social mobility. Islamist groups responded to the needs and aspirations of the newly urban who might be university students, professionals, shopkeepers, merchants, or workers. The groups offered food to the needy, scholarships and hostels to university students, a network to young graduates looking for jobs, and credit to shopkeepers, industrialists and merchants. Self-help projects conducted by women were particularly important to this endeavour. Financial assistance came from a newly formed Islamist business elite.

In the late 1980s, a new urban middle class and business elite emerged whose members often originated from provincial towns. Their parents were often self-employed small traders, small shopkeepers, merchants and agrarian capitalists. Some of them came from state employed families. Many provincial youngsters from this background moved to big cities where they had access to higher education. Since their graduation, many joined the urban middle class through employment in the modern economic sector, which expanded in the 1980s as a result of economic reforms that replaced the statist economic model with a liberal approach.

The liberal and export-oriented economic development model adopted by then Prime Minister Turgut Ozal gave birth to a new business elite, also originating from a provincial background. This new model provided opportunities not only to the established business elite, but also to the small and medium businessmen in Anatolian towns. Some of them have developed their business there. Others moved to Istanbul, seeking opportunities for expansion in this new commercial center.

Originating from Anatolian towns, the new business elite desired to assert their provincial identity and preserve their values and traditions. Consequently, they have been called "Anatolian Lions" ("Anadolu Aslanlari"), differentiating themselves from the more urban, Westernized business elite represented by TUSIAD (The Turkish Businessmen's and Industrialists' Association, founded in 1971), whose members are the chief executives of Turkey's 300 biggest corporations. In contrast, the Anatolian Lions went under the leadership of the pro-Islamist MUSIAD and now challenge the established business elite.

MUSIAD, the Association of the Independent Industrialists and Businessmen, was founded on May 5, 1990 in Istanbul by a number of young pro-Islamic businessmen: Erol Yarar (12) who was the president until May 1999, Ali Bayramolu who replaced Yarar in May 1999, Natik Akyol, and Abdurrahman Esmerer. The first letter of its acronym, "M" is commonly perceived as standing for "Muslim" rather than for mustakil ("independent"). The founders of

MUSIAD aimed to create an "Islamic economic system" as an alternative to the existing "capitalist system" in Turkey.

This goal, though, remained only a slogan. The group's membership reached 400 in 1991, 1700 by 1993, and 3000 in 1998. (13) Its members' companies' annual revenue is US $ 2.79 billion. Members are active in most sectors of the economy, particularly in manufacturing, textiles, chemical and metallurgical products, automotive parts, building materials, iron and steel, and food products. There are also several powerful Islamist finance houses. MUSIAD aims to increase its membership to 5000 and number of branch offices from 28 to 40 by the year 2000.

The Virtue Party

A new party, the Virtue Party (FP), was founded by 33 former RP deputies under the leadership of Recai Kutan on December 17, 1997. At that time it had 144 seats in the parliament which it had obtained as a result of the switchover of the RP deputies. The party's conservative wing controlled by Erbakan elected the parliamentary group leaders before the reformist wing, led by then-Istanbul Mayor Recep Tayip Erdogan, could pull itself together.

However, this did not end the power struggle in the Virtue Party between the party's young reformists and those loyal to Necmettin Erbakan, the leader of the now defunct Welfare Party. It went on, and resulted in the resignation of four (Cemil Cicek, Ali Coskun, Abduallah Gul, and Abdulkadir Aksu) of the reformists on July 26, 1999. Their resignation was interpreted as a move to form a new party given the fact that the Constitutional Court opened a closure case against the Virtue Party after the April 18, 1999 elections on the charges that the party was carrying out anti-secular activities and was the sucessor of the RP. However, they denied any plan to form a new party in their July 1999 press statements.

Prior to the 1999 local and general elections, the Virtue Party set up an organization in all districts of the country, then began recruiting new members. (26) It renewed its membership profile. According to the law, a newly founded party that replaced a banned political party shall omit 50 percent of the total membership of the now defunct party.The Virtue Party went even farther and it renewed 60 percent of members who were recruited by the now defunct Welfare Party.

Along with renewing its membership, the Virtue Party has tried to rectify its image as anti-women and un-democratic. It recruited a number of highly educated, upper middle class modern women, for example, Nazli Ilicak and Prof. Dr. Oya Akgonenc. Women from lower social classes carried the party to power, and were able to participate in public life as result of the party. But, despite their contribution, they were not invited to be represented at the higher ranks. The Virtue Party appointed Ilicak, Akgonenc and Gulten Celik as female members of the Central Decisionmaking Board. Only Celik wears a head covering.

Both Turkey's leaders and the party's own supporters ask how the FP differs from the RP. The Virtue Party has signaled that it takes some new approaches. For example, the FP declared support for Turkey's European Union membership, a step the RP opposed for three decades. An additional change was the FP's appointment of two women-who do not wear headcoverings-to its Central Decisionmaking Board. The Welfare Party demanded its supporters observe an Islamic dress code. Indeed, the FP has downplayed the headcovering issue altogether. Third, instead of mentioning the old party's "Islamic mission" its rhetoric emphasizes democracy, human rights, and personal liberty. The FP presents the headscarf ban issue as a matter of human rights violation and suppression of personal liberties rather than as a matter of religion.

Another change in the Virtue Party's rhetoric is its highlighting of the theme of "millet," (nation) as opposed to the RP's strong organic link between "millet" and "devlet" (state). The implication in the Virtue Party's stance is that the state should be in the service of the people rather than-in the RP's view-a holy state that stands far above the people. (29) The FP pledges to create a humanitarian state that meets the millet's needs without totally dominating it, a more democratic rather than more authoritarian state. This issue has become a dominant topic in articles published by Milli Gazette since January 1998, and several conferences discussed this question.

Another interesting development is the FP's position on the "Kurdish issue" is that the RP had not been hesitant to talk about Kurdish identity and the cultural rights of the Kurds without seeming to go further in backing bigger demands. The FP's chairman, Recai Kutan, spoke in favor of "cultural rights", announcing in August 1998, "It would be necessary to recognize some of the rights of Turkey's Kurdish identity. The right to educate and publish in the Kurdish language would have to be considered after discussions and a normalization period." (30) However, the FP became more cautious after the capture of the outlawed PKK leader, Abdullah Ocalan, in February 1999.

The FP has tried to change its image in a number of ways. For example, rather than holding sexually segregated social gatherings, as they did in the past, it organizes dinner parties where men and women mix freely (e.g., Nazli Ilicak and Recai Kutan sang together at a dinner party in 1998). While such an endeavor alienates religiously conservative supporters, party leaders understand the necessity of improving the party's image and making concessions.

Islamism has grown as a response to social, economic, and political discontent in Turkey, including foreign influences, urbanization, modernization, and secularization. The Islamist movement's upsurge, the growth of ultra-nationalism, and Kurdish ethno-nationalism has eroded the center in Turkey. The center-right parties have declined because they did not meet their constituency's needs or expectations, and also failed to absorb the compromising sprit of democratic liberalism.

In the context of modern Turkish political history, the Welfare and Virtue parties must be understood not only in terms of their specific Islamist ideology but also as the representative of specific social sectors reacting to circumstances. Equally, and partly as a result of this fact, the erosion of the center-right and increased support given to the Islamist and the ultra-nationalist parties has not yet created the danger of regime instability. (31) The nationalist secular majority in Turkey (32), supporters of the DSP and other parties, counterweight the Islamist and ultra-nationalist groups in both public life and in parliament.

Milli Gorus

Milli Gorus ("National View") is a non-nationalist and pan-Islamic movement of political Islam. The father of the movement was former Turkish prime minister Necmettin Erbakan, who was ousted by the military. Erbakan's three subsequent political parties (Nizam, Fazilet and Refah) were all outlawed. Prime Minister Erdogan and the AKP are the offspring of this political Islamist movement.

During the 1950s, the Islamist movement began to grow as a potent political force through the establishment of an Islamic-based political party. Clashes with secularist institutions, particularly the military, resulted in the Islamist parties being banned from political participation. Islamist political participation, however, continued to grow, and new parties formed to replace banned predecessors. Following the 1980 military coup, Necemettin Erbakan established the Welfare Party. By the 1990s, the Welfare party had gained sufficient electoral support needed to establish a coalition government and elevate Erbakan to the office of Prime Minister.

Within the Welfare Party, Cakir identified two main ideological currents: a traditionalist view, advocated by Erbakan, and a modernist view, which was championed by Recep Tayyip Erdogan, the mayor of Istanbul. Traditionalists used Islamic institutions and Islam in general to form their core support. Modernists, however, actively sought to incorporate those previously on the periphery, particularly women, youth, and the unemployed, into their political base. Modernist Welfare members were not less religious than traditionalists—to the contrary, modernists were more influenced by other Islamist movements in the region.

Following the "postmodern coup d'etat" in 1997 that resulted in the removal and banning of the Welfare Party, the modernist faction began to redefine itself in order to become compatible with the realities of a secular political system. Erdogan and other younger members of the Welfare Party began to criticize openly the party's past, and depicted themselves as conservative instead of Islamist. To build support for their new approach, Erdogan sought legitimacy for the new movement abroad. In the years following Welfare's demise, Erdogan and others traveled throughout the United States and Europe meeting with diplomats, government officials, and others with interests in the region.

Departing from the position held by the Welfare Party, Erdogan championed Turkey's movement toward membership in the European Union and actively sought to strengthen political and economic ties with the United States and Europe. Cakir believes that Erdogan's European overtures, which occurred at a time when the West was aware of the eventual collapse of the fragile coalition government formed in 1999, allowed Erdogan and other modernists to achieve the legitimacy necessary to form their own political party, the AK Party.

Once in power, the AK Party positioned themselves as "conservative democrats," although Cakir contended that the party had no other feasible option within the current secularist political system. Determined to avoid the fate of its Islamist predecessors, the AK Party has depicted itself as a national party not based solely on regional, ethnic, or religious support. Erdogan, as Prime Minister, has been a vocal champion of both Turkey's accession into the EU and domestic reforms, and according to Cakir the AK Party has been far more progressive on these issues than other Turkish parties.

Until now, however, Erdogan and the AK Party have largely ignored problems related to Turkish secularism. To illustrate this, Cakir examined the headscarf debate, which stems from a longstanding ban on women being allowed to wear head scarves in public buildings. Many within AK's base, particularly devout Muslim women, strongly support removing the ban, but Erdogan and other AK Party leaders have hitherto refused to address this issue. To the contrary, Erdogan has publicly stated that resolution of the headscarf debate is not his main agenda. Cakir believes that the AK Party has been very sensible in bypassing sensitive issues related to secularism, which has allowed the party to focus on the EU question and related reforms

Recep Tayip Erdogan

The scholar period

Erdoğan was born in Kasımpaşa, Istanbul. His family was descended from Georgian immigrants who settled from Batum to Rize. (During his visit to Georgia in 2004, he pronounced his origins.) Erdoğan spent his early childhood in Rize before returning to Istanbul at the age of 13. He was educated at a religious Imam Hatip school and at Marmara University's Faculty of Economics and Administrative Sciences (İktisadi ve İdari Bilimler Fakültesi) . Erdoğan played semi-professional football for 16 years.

The political carrier

In the 27 March 1994 local elections, Erdoğan was hand-picked by Erbakan for his oratory skills and was elected mayor with the party ticket. The Welfare Party became the largest party in Turkey for the first time, and Erdoğan became Mayor of Greater Istanbul as well as President of the Greater Istanbul Metropolitan Council.

As Mayor of Istanbul, he made a name for himself as a populist, effective administrator, building up Istanbul's infrastructure and transportation grid, while simultaneously beautifying the city, becoming one of Turkey's most popular politicians in the process. During this period Turkish Islamist politics entered a period of chaos.

Imprisonment

Erdoğan's pro-Islamist sympathies earned him a conviction in 1998. As the Istanbul Mayor, Erdogan was the most prominent mayor over 200 mayors and other officials in Turkey; because he was a national figure and hero to millions of Islamic-oriented voters, his case has focused attention.

In 1997, the Welfare Party was declared unconstitutional and was shut down on the grounds of threatening the secular nature of the state. In 1998, Erdoğan become a constant speaker at the meetings that was established by his friends from the banned Welfare Party. The secularism in Turkey is taken very seriously since the establishment of the state with the Kemalist Ideology as its guiding principle. Aligned with the Atatürk's Reforms the

Constitution of Turkey states that laïcité, social equality, equality before law are the main and unchangeable characteristics of the Turkey.

Kemalist ideology also adapted the position of "public reason", which claimed that activities falling outside of the private sphere should be secular and no religious group should be given permission to dominate over other belief systems. Any activity or promotion of activity of domination over other belief systems are perceived under somewhat a controversial concept of "incitement to religious hatred," which has been in of Turkish constitution as "religious hatred" since its establishment. The "religious hatred" concept has been used against the movements which promoted the reinstitution of caliphate through the reestablishment of the abolished Ottoman Caliphate and Islamic fundamentalist positions.

There is no question that Erdogan is a pro-Islamist [calls himself religious conservative] but the extent of his position regarding to basic characteristics of the state [secularism] has been questioned on 12 December 1997 at a public meeting in Siirt in Eastern Anatolia. In his speech, Erdoğan identified the Turkish society as having "two fundamentally different camps" -- those who blindly fallow the Atatürk's Reforms [seculars] and the Muslims who unite Islam with Sharia. He publicly read a well-known an Islamic poem including modified lines:

The AKP

The disbanded Welfare Party promptly reformed itself under a new name, the Virtue Party (Fazilet Partisi), which in turn was found unconstitutional on the same grounds in 1999.

Erdogan become the leader of a faction of moderate conservative members within the old Welfare Party, known as English, Reformist ("Yenilikçiler") formed the Justice and Development Party on August 14, 2001, in an attempt to ground moderate conservative politics in a secular democratic framework. Erdoğan, stated that "AKP is not a political party with a religious axis." when the party was founded. On the other side, the traditionalists formed the Felicity Party (Saadet Partisi).

Privatization

Erdoğan's success story is keeping the economy on the track as designed by the Kemal Dervis. Erdoğan supported the Ali Babacan, which Babacan continued to enforce the macro economic policies of Kemal Dervis. Erdoğan did not cut the relations to international monitory control systems in favor of a national economy. The AK Party did quite well in almost all areas of the economy apart from the account deficit. Erdoğan said that during this premiership the economy's average growth rate was 7.3%, capita annual income had almost doubled, and all these were related to his economic reforms and the pursue of the membership of the European Union. However Erdogan's polices on unemployment figures were not effective.

Islamisation

Since Prime Minister Erdogan's AKP (Justice and Development Party) came to power in 2002, the rift between Turkey's secular circles and the government on many issues has deepened, often due to remarks by PM Erdogan himself.

Erdogan's statements on Turkish identity occupied the public agenda throughout December 2005. First, he defined Turkey's ethnic groups as its "sub-identities," with "citizenship in Turkey." His refusal to accept "Turkish" as the supra-identity of the people of Turkey, and his rejection of the concept of "the Turkish nation," sparked furious reactions from Turkey's secularist and nationalist circles.

Then, in response to a question about Turkey's Kurdish minority (during an official visit to New Zealand), Erdogan said that Turkey's dozens of ethnic groups were tied together by their shared religion - meaning Islam: "Turkey is 99% Muslim, and above all, it is our religion that ties us all together." Upon his return to Turkey, he clarified his statements: "I did not say that Islam is our supra-identity [as the media reported]. I said that Islam is the cement, and the most important factor, uniting our people."

While the Islamist media in Turkey hailed Erdogan's expression of these views, the secular media protested, stressing that the Turkish people's only higher identity was Turkish citizenship in the secular Turkish republic.

On December 10, Oktay Eksi wrote in *Hurriyet*: "*This is a friendly warning. [...] The ruling AKP government is following a very wrong and dangerous path. They [the AKP] are in an overall offensive against [our] secular Republic. They used to say, 'We respect the Law.' Then, when they were displeased with the law in Turkey, they carried it to the European Court of Human Rights*

[ECHR]. When they did not like the results of the Leyla Sahin case, they defied the ECHR and the law.

"They used to say that they respected science. Yet they launched an all-out war against the [Turkish] Higher Education Council and the universities. [...] In dealing with the European Union [membership] criteria, they kept saying 'one flag, one nation, one homeland' - but they changed, very quickly, 'one nation' into 'one ummet' [umma]."

On the subject of Prime Minister Erdogan's definition of Islam as the "cement" of the people of Turkey, opposition CHP (Republican People's Party) member of parliament Ali Topuz was quoted in most of Turkey's mainstream newspapers: *"[...] If religion [Islam] is the cement of our people, what are we supposed to do about our non-Muslim minorities [and] the atheists? Are we going to exclude them from our nation? [...] The prime minister must remember that Ataturk brought us secularism, and absolute separation of state and religion is one of the most important principles of the Turkish revolution. [...] I call on the prime minister to demonstrate political maturity."*

On December 18, 2005 Hayrettin Karaman wrote in the Islamic daily *Yeni Safak*: *"[...] Being a Muslim demands the subordination of tribalism (which corresponds to nationalism in today's language) to the unity of Islamic brotherhood. Islam comes above all other ties. [...] When the Islamic nation (umma) is united, no Muslim individual or group will be left out; they will be part of it. [...] According to the Lausanne treaty, only the non-Muslims are recognized as minorities in Turkey."*

On December 11, Murat Bardakci wrote in the secular mass-circulation daily *Hurriyet*: *"[...] If what the prime minister said were true, and that religion was such an important uniting factor, how come we [Turks], during the collapse of the Ottoman Empire, were bitterly betrayed by Muslims [...] and why was it that the [bloody] uprisings during the initial years of our republic were by the [rebelling] religious [Muslims]? [...] In 1914, at the outset of the [First] World War, wasn't it Hussein, the sharif of Mecca, who issued the fatwas against the Ottoman Sultan-Caliph Reshad inciting all Arabs to a rebellion that painted the Muslim lands with the blood of tens of thousands of [our] sons? [...] In 1925, Sheikh Said issued calls from southeast Anatolia to arm and attack the Turks: [...] '...Capture their soldiers, [...] the infidel Turks' cannons, the Turks' guns [...]. Your guide is Mohammed, your helper is Allah. You are many times stronger than their government [in Ankara] [...] Save and protect the sanctity of Islam [...]'"*

Since the ascension to power of Turkish Prime Minister Recep Tayyip Erdogan's AK Party in 2002, there has been a rift between the government and Turkey's Higher Education Council (YOK) on various issues.

Prior to the 2002 election, the AKP promised its Islamic electorate that it would end the ban on Islamic headscarves in the universities, and that the graduates of Turkey's Imam Hatip religious schools would be accepted into the universities.

However, once in office, the ruling AKP could not deliver on these promises to its religious base, mainly because of the strong opposition on the part of Turkey's strictly secular Higher Education Council that governs the policies of Turkey's state universities. The conflict deepened with the recent arrest and incarceration of the president of Yuzuncu Yil University (YYU) in Van, Professor Yucel Askin, for alleged procedural misconduct.

The Turkish media is suggesting that Prof. Askin's incarceration was an attempt by the Islamic government to remove a secular republican president from a university that was known, until he took office in 1999, as a hotbed for Islamists. During his tenure, Prof. Askin put an end to the activities of various Islamic extremists at the university.

All Turkey's university presidents, as well as the Higher Education Council and members of the Turkish Bar Associations, strongly protested Prof. Askin's arrest, and claimed that Turkey's judiciary system was being manipulated by the government. On October 22, 2005, 74 presidents and vice-presidents of Turkish universities flew to Van to visit Prof. Askin in prison, in a show of solidarity, and held a meeting at YYU. A declaration by the Board of Presidents of YOK read: "Defending President Askin means defending our Republic." Higher Education Council head Professor E. Tezic and the 74 presidents were met by a number of protesters in Van, who shouted "Allahu Akbar."

Soon after their visit to Van, President of the Turkish Republic Ahmet N. Sezer invited all the university presidents to his October 29 Republic Day Reception, further angering Prime Minister Erdogan, who earlier had said about the solidarity visit, "Those who go to Van [i.e. the university presidents] should mind their own businesses and not interfere with legal matters."

Erdogan on Secularism:

"*If the people want it, of course secularism will go away. You cannot rule this people by force; you don't have the power to do that. This [i.e. secularism] cannot work in spite of the people. And anyway, for the love of Allah, what is this secularism? You ask them to define it. They can't. They say that it varies from place to place. So what sort of a strange thing is this [secularism]? Today, for every concept there is a definition in the dictionary. Every concept must have a definition [...]*

The interior minister comes and says that the state can interfere with religion. What about the rest? Why don't you say the rest? No! He does not say that the religion can interfere with the state. Yesterday I was at the Bosphorus University; and some of the - probably impressionable - young people there asked me, 'Mr. Mayor, what do you think about secularism? There are concerns that secularism is disappearing. What will happen?' This is what I said to those young friends:

'In the West they say, Render unto Caesar the things which are Caesar's, and unto God the things that are God's. But this country's interior minister says that Caesar has rights but God does not!' But the fact is that 99% of the people of this country are Muslims. You cannot be both secular and a Muslim! You will either be a Muslim, or secular! When both are together, they create reverse magnetism [i.e. they repel one another]. For them to exist together is not a possibility! Therefore, it is not possible for a person who says 'I am a Muslim' to go on and say 'I am secular too.' And why is that? Because Allah, the creator of the Muslim, has absolute power and rule!"

Erdogan on Turkish Constitution:

"*As for [the motto of Turkish democracy] 'Sovereignty belongs unconditionally to the people.' Now, look here. This is a lie! And it's a huge lie! We [former PM Erbakan's Islamist RP (Welfare) Party] suggested this to them for their constitution: We said 'Let's put brackets next to 'sovereignty belongs unconditionally to the people' and write within the brackets, 'once every five years.'*

They began to laugh. I asked them why they were laughing. Do the people have such a privilege, other than once every five years? Then what's-his-name says - and where does he say this? - it is in 1985 and we are having a discussion on the constitution in a meeting in the Marmara Hotel. He gets up and says 'No, this is not right.'

At that moment, the former finance minister, who was completely drunk, also joins in to give advice. I told them that they must have prepared this constitution at the same table [at which they together consume alcohol]. Why? Because they do not prepare these constitutions with sober heads, but with drunken heads! That is why their constitutions last no more than two years.

Now, this constitution is full of gaps and holes. Like a rag with patches. The other day journalists asked me what I think about this [constitution]. I said, Look, what do they say? That sovereignty belongs unconditionally to the people. You must think well. When [does the sovereignty belong to the people]? It is only when they go to the polls [every five years] that sovereignty belongs to the people. But both materially, and in essence, sovereignty unconditionally and always belongs to Allah!"

Erdogan and the women

Speaking yesterday at a conference in Istanbul entitled "Woman and Politics," Emine Erdogan, the wife of Prime Minister Recep Tayyip Erdogan, said that women are inevitable participants in politics as in life. "Our women have to undertake responsibilities in politics just as they have at home," said Erdogan. Commenting on the number of candidates fielded by her husband's ruling Justice and Development Party (AKP) for upcoming local elections, Erdogan called the number regrettably inadequate, adding that the prime minister felt the same way. /Cumhuriyet/

To better understand the tension between East and West in the Muslim world, this report, "Muslims," travelled to Istanbul, Turkey -- a city straddling both Europe and Asia.

Istanbul has a rich Islamic past. Until 1922, it was the center of the last great Islamic empire of the Ottomans. But in 1923, Kemal Ataturk became the first leader of a Muslim people to believe that in order to modernize, Islam's influence on society had to be crushed.

Under Ataturk, Friday ceased to be a public holiday, and mosques emptied. Sharia law was replaced by Western legal codes. Islamic scholars were forced under state control. Arabic script was replaced by the Latin alphabet. European dress was required for both men and women.

By the 1970s, Turkey had become the most Westernized of Muslim countries and an active member of NATO. But at the same time, rapid urbanization was changing Turkey's cities, and a free market economy had increased inequality. Voters were frustrated at what they saw as corruption within the political system. Many Muslims began to question Ataturk's belief that Islam should be removed from politics. Pro-Islamic politicians promised to rectify a split that they saw as artificial.

By 1996, a Turkish Islamic party had gained enough popularity to win over 20 percent of the national vote and came to power in a coalition government. In response, secular officials clamped down on Islam's most visible symbols, among them the head scarf.

Fethullah Gulen

The Gulen movement is attracting increasing and sometimes hostile attention both inside Turkey and beyond as a result of its increasing activity, wealth, and influence. Inspired by the thoughts of its founder, Sufi scholar Fethullah Gulen, it has established hundreds of educational institutions, as well as media outlets, dialogue platforms, and charities. Well-established in Turkey, it has expanded into the wider Turkic world and, increasingly, beyond. Yet its structure, ambitions, and size remain opaque, making assessment of its impact and power difficult.

Introduction

Recent developments have led to an upsurge of curiosity about the Turkish Sufi scholar Fethullah Gulen and his legion of followers, known as Fethullahci, both in his native country and abroad. One factor contributing to this attention was Gulen's summer 2008 election as the world's leading intellectual in a poll organized jointly by the British Prospect magazine and the U.S. publication Foreign Policy, in which over half a million votes were registered for a candidate who had hitherto been unknown to Prospect's editor.

Prospect's analysis of the poll highlighted how relatively high levels of Turkish internet use generated a specifically Turkish effect in such polls.Prospect also identified in Gulen's victory theemergence of a new kind of intellectual, "one whose influence is expressed through a personal network, aided by theinternet, rather than publications or institutions."

These observations offer a penetrating insight into the mechanisms of Gulen's influence and the nature of the Gulen movement.

Prospect additionally noted how votes for Gulen mounted in the wake of publicity for the poll in the Gulen-inspired Turkish newspaper Zaman and a host of other Gulen websites. This testified to the legendary "efficiency and discipline" and "organizational ability" of the Fethullahci.

There is a hint of something sinister in this interpretation of Gulen's victory, implying as it does central direction rather than spontaneity. Secular Turks share such suspicions, and conspiracy theories abound in Turkey concerning both the source and level of the movement's funding and the nature of its ultimate ambitions.

Indeed, both are obscure. It is often alleged that the Gulen movement receives funding, either alternatively or simultaneously, from the CIA, Saudi Arabia, Iran, and the Turkish state.

Gulen himself has lived in somewhat hermit-like exile in Pennsylvania since 1998, ostensibly due to ill-health but also as a consequence of fears for his freedom should he return to Turkey. He was charged in 1999 for "establishing an illegal organization in order to change the secular structure of the state and to establish a state based on religious rules."

Although he was acquitted in 2006, the judgment was appealed, and it was not until June 2008 that the acquittal was finally upheld, thus clearing the way for his safe returnto Turkey.

In the West, most would probably concur with The Economist, which has noted the generally good reception received there by the Gulen movement, whose security services "have not detected any hidden ties with extremism."

On the other hand, according to the American "neo-conservative" Michael Rubin, if Gulen does return to Turkey "Istanbul 2008 may very well look like Tehran 1979."Rubin anticipates millions turning out to greet Gulen on his return to Turkey, his issuing of fatwas (religious edicts) designed to distance Turkey from its official secularism, the restoration of the caliphate, and the subversion of the rule of law "to an imam's conception of God."

In more measured fashion, Hakan Yavuz, a U.S.-based Turkish scholar of Islam in Turkey, has been quoted as asserting that the Gulen movement is "the most powerful movement right now in the country.... The point where they are today scares me. There is no other movement to balance them in society."

The movement's activities abroad sometimes arouse comparable suspicions. The Russian authorities, fearful of any indications of Islamic or pan-Turkic revivalism within their borders, have recently tried to close down a Gulen school in St. Petersburg as part of a wider campaign against the movement's activities and influences, a campaign which has included bans on the works of the Sufi teacher Said Nursi, from whom Gulen draws much of his inspiration.

In light of all this, it is interesting to note that the U.S. authorities chose to reject Gulen's application for the right of permanent residence in the United States on the grounds of his insufficient renown, a decision ruled improper by a federal judge in July 2008.

Clearly Gulen and the Fethullahciare divisive, but they have also been described by The Economist as "one of the most powerful and best-connected of the networks that are competing to influence Muslims round the globe." In addition to its global activism, the movement constitutes a major part of Turkey's current social and political evolution, signified by the electoral fortunes of the ruling Justice and Development Party (Adalet ve Kalkinma Partisi, AKP), with which it overlaps.

Yet it remains opaque. This article will seek to throw such light as can be thrown on the movement, and offer a critical assessment of its values, nature, and impact. It will in part draw on this author's experiences and observations during a week spent in Istanbul in July 2008 as a guest of the Gulen-inspired and UK-based Dialogue Society (http://www.dialoguesociety.org), during which various aspects of the ideas and activities of the movement were discussed, and Gulen-inspired businessmen's associations, media outlets, educational establishments, and the like were visited.

Gulen's Thinking

One cannot understand the nature of the movement without some mention of Fethullah Gulen's thinking. Although this has evolved towards more universalistic, pluralistic, liberal, and democratic values, in large measure it remains rooted in Turkey's particular circumstances and experiences. For Gulen, Kemalist Turkey's "top-down" imposition of a dogmatic secularism has distanced swathes of Turkish society from the governing elite. Gulen prefers to draw inspiration from the Ottoman model of state-society relationships. Although the empire's rulers were guided by their faith, the Ottoman system of governance was not theocratic. Public laws were formulated on the basis of the state's needs rather than in accordance with Islamic law (Shari'a). For Gulen, the state has a functionally secular responsibility to provide internal and external security and stability for its citizens. Gulen's state-centrism even led him to sympathize with Turkey's 1980 military coup, regarding it as appropriate that the state protect itself and its citizens against the chaos that was threatening to engulf Turkish society.

Thus, Gulen is not in favor of the political implementation of Shari'a, though the freedom to express one's faith should be respected. He is opposed to "political Islam," and even sympathized with Turkey's 1997 "post-modern coup" that removed Necmettin Erbakan's Welfare Party from power, although Gulen was himself caught up in the crackdown on religious activity that came in its wake. He believed that Erbakan and his followers were embarked on the first steps towards an "Iranianization" of Turkish political and social life.

Gulen believes that there is no necessary contradiction between Islam and modernity. Indeed, Turkish Islam's more adaptable and less doctrinal Sufi traditions have enabled Turkey, with its democratization, free market economy, and secular political system, to incorporate aspects of modernity barely found elsewhere in the Muslim world.

A key to his thinking is that Islam should positively embrace science, reason, democratization, and tolerance. It should not shield itself from other faiths, other ideas, or from scientific and technological progress. Gulen believes that the relative (to the West) economic and moral poverty of so much of the Islamic world is explained by its attachment to misplaced and dogmatic interpretations of Islam, not Islam per se. Indeed, he believes Turkey can lead the Islamic world toward this realization, and for all his proclaimed universalism there is also a pronounced "Turkishness" to his thinking. Turkish society is nationalistic, and some of this flavor has been absorbed by Gulen and the Fethullahci.

For Gulen, the key to Islam's adaptation to the modern world does not lie in direct political activity and organization. Rather, Gulen propagates a kind of "educational Islamism" as opposed to a "political Islamism."

Thus, educational curricula should emphasize science, technology, and instruction in the English language. In place of faith teaching Gulen advocates the cultivation of spiritual, moral, and behavioral values, of tolerance, respect, openness, and the like. Indeed, Gulen feels that the West has forsaken the spiritual dimension of human existence.

Through the internalized spiritual transformation of individuals, a wider social transformation will evolve and, indirectly, a (re-) "Islamized" version of modernity. Thus, politics should be "Islamized" only via a bottom-up process and indirectly, in which people and state are reconnected through a shared attachment to and internalization of values.

It is an approach that resembles a kind of "long march through the institutions." In this sense, Gulen's mission can be said to be a political project, but one that aspires to achieve its goals indirectly. People of faith as well as learning, a "Golden Generation," should be cultivated andencouraged to dedicate their lives to the service (hizmet)of the people and to inspire them towards the movement's objectives.

The emphasis on spirituality in Gulen's thinking is partly explained by his attachment to Turkey's "folk Islam," Sufism. Specifically, Gulen derives inspiration from the writings of the prominent Kurdish religious authority Said Nursi (1877-1961).

His Nur (Light) movement was similarly distinguished by its advocacy of reason, progress, and tolerance, and its quietism towards direct political involvement. Even if Turkish Islam's uniqueness is sometimes exaggerated, there is little doubt that its sects, saints, and eclecticism can be offensive to other Muslims, as can its "moderation."

Sufism also typically features the kind of master-disciple relationships replicated today by the inspiration Gulen provides his followers. Widespread membership of Sufi sects has long persisted in secular Turkey, generally concealed from the country's suspicious rulers.

Gulen has also advocated both local and global interfaith and inter-civilizational dialogue, and to this end met with Pope John Paul II in Rome in 1998, and inside Turkey with Patriarch Bartholomeos, head of the Greek Orthodox Fener Patriarchate in Istanbul, the former Chief Rabbi of Turkey's Jewish community David Aseo, as well as with numerous other high-profile Jewish and Christian figures.[18] In its support for and sponsorship of such activities, the Gulen movement seeks both to counter the impact of the more violent fundamentalist strains in modern Islam -- Gulen has repeatedly condemned terrorism as "un-Islamic"--and to undermine wherever it can Huntington's "Clash of Civilizations"
thesis.

Gulen's championing of interfaith dialogue springs in part from his recognition of the shared theological originsof Islam, Christianity, and Judaism--although in his appeal for interfaith dialogue and tolerance

Gulen incorporates Buddhism and Hinduism too--and Muhammad's injunction to respect the "people of the book." The transcendental quality of faith is for Gulen a unifying force that outweighs theological differences. His commitment to dialogue with the Judeo-Christian world is also related to his admiration for Western modernity, liberalism, and technological and economic prowess. Gulen's frequent and approving references to the "Global Village" express his perception that the phenomena of globalization have so bound together the fates of peoples that conflict between them serves nobody's interests.

Characteristically, he again draws upon the multifaith and multicultural example of the Ottoman Empire, which he adduces as evidence of the capacity of diverse peoples to live together harmoniously. The flavor of Gulen's thinking is then distinctly moderate, and offers little credence to some of the wilder accusations against him; but what of the movement that takes his name?

The Fethullahci

In the wake of Gulen's appointment as a state-employed religious preacher to Izmir in 1966, a loose network of students, teachers, professionals, businessmen, and the like began to gather around him and to coalesce as a spontaneous "social movement" inspired by Gulen's example.

Its first venture into the wider propagation of its philosophy came in the form of summer schools, from which it progressed to the establishment of teaching centers (dershane),often dormitories, to prepare religious students for university admission. These remain an important element in the inculcation of Gulen's values, not least through a "mentoring" system found throughout the movement's educational establishments and its wider "structure."

The dershane are also a prime source of recruits. As it blossomed, so it attracted the attention of Turkey's secularist state establishment. Gulen himself served a seven-month spell in prison in the early 1970s for propagating religion, and again attracted uncomfortable attention both during the 1980s and, as already noted, in the late 1990s. The network did not openly blossom as a major educational, social, and religious movement until the early 1980s, when in the wake of the military coup of 1980 the space for religious activity was expanded, a policy inspired by the so-called "Turkish-Islamic synthesis." This advocated a fusion between Turkish national identity and the Islamic faith, in the hope that a (state- managed) religiosity would offer a politically less threatening antidote to the leftism that had contributed to the social chaos of the preceding decade.

It has been argued that "the rural and pious masses of Anatolia remained largely unaffected by the cultural re-engineering" of Kemalism, and that Turkey has remained a "torn" society a la Huntington. The wider "democratization" and opening up of social, economic, and political life in Turkey after 1983 reinforced this "center-periphery" encapsulation of Turkish politics and society.

Turkey's increased pluralism has enabled its more devout and conservative provincial hinterland to challenge the Kemalist, secular, "Westernizing" and urban center.This ideological rift has been reinforced by the ascendance of a more traditional, pious Anatolian business and professional class. The Gulen movement also profited from this post-1980 liberalization, which created a space for its media, educational, and financial activities free from the controlof the statist secular establishment and which was accompanied by, and contributed to, a more general "Islamization" of Turkish public life.

Turkey's "new" class of businessmen, professionals, teachers, and intellectuals form the core of the Fethullahci. Thismiddle class profile is not quite coincident with the newly-urbanized working class or the rural poor who provide thebackbone of the AKP's electoral support.

Gulen followers range from extremely pious individuals--often teachers andpreachers and those engaged in the movement's dialogue activities, who are inspired by the Islamic principle of hizmet, andwhose lives are dedicated to the propagation of the values and ideas of Fethullah Gulen--to the more occasional and morepragmatic sympathizers, such as businessmen, politicians, journalists, and increasingly even officials of the supposedlysecular Kemalist state.

Collectively, these might be regarded as Gulen's "Golden Generation." The movement's pious activists are inclined towards constant and somewhat uncritical reference to Gulen's writings. Such "true believers" canconvey the impression of "cultism," and can perhaps be likened to early Christian sects, certainly in their motivation but perhaps also in their spontaneity.

There seems little reason to doubt the debt of the movement's business backers to Gulen's philosophy, the sincerity of their Islamic approach to their wider social and moral obligations, their desire to please God, and their voluntarism. Zakat is one of the five pillars of Islam, and obliges Muslims to donate 2.5 percent of their wealth to worthy causes. Sadaqa, or voluntary charity, can inspire the wealthy to donate in excess of this minimum.

Many rich Gulen sympathizers do indeed donate a large percentage of their personal wealth, as expressions of their commitment. Businessmen, typically forming tightly-knit circles drawn from a particular town or locality and whose relationships rely heavily on mutual trust, donate--in money or in kind--to the building of schools and the like as acts of Islamic charity. Such "giving" might also bring a commercial return in the form of contracts or "profits" from a venture's revenue-raising capacity,[25] although the general principle is that ventures should be self-financing and that any surplus funds be ploughed back.

Initially benefitting from some protective cover from Prime Minister Turgut Ozal, reckoned to be a sympathizer, the movement has since gone on to open around 200 schools in Turkey since its first was established in 1982, universities such as Fatih in Istanbul, hospitals, charities, a television channel (Samanyolu TV)--which now has plans to broadcast to the Turkish community in Germany--a radio station (Burc FM), a mass-circulation daily newspaper (Zaman)--which in addition to its online English-language edition also publishes elsewhere in the Turkic world such as Azerbaijan, Kyrgyzstan, Turkmenistan and Bashkortostan in the Russian Federation--and several other periodicals.

In 1996 it established a bank, Asya Finans, operating on the basis of Islamic principles such as interest-free banking and initially tasked to raise investment funds for the newly-independent Turkic republics. Its activities are now extensive and global.

The network also spawned a Journalists and Writers Foundation (http://www.gyv.org.tr/), largely to facilitate dialogue activities, and a Teachers Foundation, each of which publishes journals and organizes symposiums and conferences-- frequently abroad--and provides an umbrella for a host of dialogue groups and charitable organizations.

Cooperation between and overlapping membership of these various institutions is extensive and confusing--largely because Gulen-inspired institutions rarely own up to that fact. The websites of its schools, universities, media outlets, charities, and dialogue groups almost never directly refer to Gulen's inspiration.

Furthermore, the movement is loosely structured and decentralized, and each of its ventures are individually financed (and usually self-financing), and run on a voluntary basis by sympathizers with the network. The movement consists of numerous businessmen's associations, education trusts, and the like--each acting independently.

Nor does it have a membership as such, and Fethullahci are often loath to declare themselves openly as such. Indeed, the distinction between members, followers, sympathizers, and collaborators is blurred, and the movement is coy about revealing its scale—which it might not accurately know. As a consequence, estimates of the movement's "membership" vary considerably. One source suggested a figure anywhere between 200,000 and four million Turks.

More recently, Prospect offered a figure of five million. This "structure," or lack of it, raises the question of whether so devolved, publicity-shy and voluntaristic a movement can exhibit the sense of purpose and discipline sometimes attributed to it, but it also adds to the suspicion with which it is regarded.

It is an internet-connected, informal and word-of-mouth set of overlapping networks that is more social movement than organization. It fuses faith with practical activity in a way that empirical and material analysis finds hard to grasp. It is undoubtedly well-resourced, interconnected, effective, and extensive, with tentacles throughout society and sympathizers within the political and bureaucratic elite. Indeed, Gulen sympathizers can increasingly be found in government service. A Turkish interior minister once suggested that as many as 70 percent of the nation's police force are Gulen sympathizers.

This is the kind of development that aggravates Turkey's secularists. After all, the judicial case against Gulen in the late 1990s was based on a tape in which he seemed to be urging his followers to take over the state by stealth. This chimes with the mission with which Gulen's "Golden Generation" is tasked--to re-Islamize society from below. Overall, the impression is of a parallel structure and society that sits uneasily alongside Turkey's officially secular state institutions and ruling elite, providing a silent, amorphous, and ungraspable challenge.

Educational activities

Overt religious teaching, and even explicit mention of Fethullah Gulen, is generally absent from Gulen educational establishments, both in Turkey and abroad. This is partly explained by the need to tread carefully in the presence of political authorities suspicious of religious (or on occasion for Gulen ventures abroad, foreign) activities.

It also reflects Gulen's educational philosophy, which stresses teaching "by example" and the cultivation of "good behavior" rather than religious devotion. In any case, matters of faith can be left to extra-curricula classes and the "mentoring" system, conducted by a teaching staff invariably made up of Gulen devotees. Gulen schools everywhere abide by local curricula, and both in Turkey and abroad they are immensely popular due to the strong reputation they have acquired for the quality of their technical and scientific teaching, for their English language instruction, and the high behavioral standards they set. This is true too of Gulen schools that serve the West's Turkish communities.

As a result, fees and entrance requirements are usually high, although schemes are sometimes in place for assisting able but poorer children.
Around half of Gulen schools are located abroad, and of those the majority are found in Turkic Central Asia and Azerbaijan, where there are also half a dozen Gulen-sponsored universities and numerous other educational, welfare, and economic institutions and activities.

Indeed, the movement's focus is on Turkic communities, including those of the Russian Federation such as Dagestan, Karachay-Cherkessia, Tatarstan, and Bashkotorstan, and other former Soviet states containing Turkic or formerly Ottoman Muslim minorities such as Ukraine, Georgia, and Moldova, and in the Balkans. One can readily see why the movement targeted Turkic Central Asia and Azerbaijan for the main thrust of its activities. After all, many in Turkey's political class made a similar assessment of Turkish prospects in the region in the immediate aftermath of the Soviet collapse.

It shares a linguistic and ethnic root with Turkey, and a "folk Islam" that, as in Turkey, incorporates numerous Sufisects and has absorbed pre-Islamic traditions, beliefs, and rituals. Furthermore, the Soviet era left behind a legacy of secular education and a commitment to science and modernity that broadly corresponds with the Gulen movement's aspirations.

The movement's activities in the wider Turkic world are additionally explained by its "commitment to Gulen's Turko- Islamic worldview." As one observer has expressed it, "...the followers of the Gulen community aspire to reconnect Central Asians with their Turkic origins by spreading Turkish Muslim culture and morality to that region."

Even in Iraq ,the Gulen schools' pupils are usually ethnic Turkmen, although Iraq's Turkmen are predominantly Shi'a rather than Sunni. Interestingly, Gulen has claimed that his movement was denied permission to open a school in an Azeri (Turkic) region of Iran due to Tehran's suspicion of its pan-Turkic aspirations.

Indeed, there may have been a greater receptivity to the "Turkism" of Gulen establishments located in Turkic regions rather than to their Islam. Turkish is used extensively, in addition to local languages where necessary. Furthermore, the overwhelming majority of the teachers and administrators in the movement's institutions abroad are Turks from Turkey rather than locals,[36] although this could change as the movement spawns indigenous Gulen devotees.

As the movement has matured, so it appears to have shifted from its Turco-centrism to "global educational activities that encourage the national identities of the countries in which it is operating." Today, Gulen schools and other educational establishments are globally far-flung, and can be found in locations as diverse as Russia, Armenia, the United States, Australia, China, Cambodia, sub-Saharan Africa, India, Pakistan, and in Western countries where Turkish minorities are located, notably Germany.

The intake of Gulen schools is mostly, though not exclusively, aimed at local Muslim populations. Interestingly though, even in decidedly non-Turkic countries such as India and in African states, portraits of Ataturk are on show, Turkish is taught, and the Turkish national anthem sung. Again, the Turkishness of Gulen schools seems more evident than their Islamism. This emphasis on Turkish language and culture has even won over some of the usually suspicious representatives of Turkey's secularist political class.

Some Gulen schools do not even have amajority Muslim intake, and might be located in zones of interreligious strife. Thus, in the Philippines, in an area wherethe denominational split between Muslims and Christians is roughly half and half, a Gulen school employs many Filipinoteachers (some of whom are Christian) and admits many Christian students.

Furthermore, and in keeping with the movement's commitment to interfaith dialogue, strong and healthy links are maintained with nearby Christian institutions.Even in Central Asia, non-Muslim students might be granted admission to Gulen establishments.

Interfaith Dialogue

Tracing the range of interfaith activities of the Gulen movement is difficult, given its devolved nature and its coy approach to self-publicity. The movement has sponsored or contributed to a confusing diversity of often overlapping interfaith organizations that operate both at the global or transnational and at the local intrasocietal level. Unsurprisingly, the Gulen movement is seen by many non-Muslims as a particularly congenial Islamic dialogue partner. Amongst the numerous U.S.- based Gulen organizations are the Institute of InterFaith Dialog (http://www.interfaithdialog.org) and the InterFaith Cultural Organization (http://www.uga.edu/ifco).

The movement takes the credit for organizing the Inter-Civilization Dialogue Conference in 1997, and in 1998, it initiated the annual Eurasian Meetings, focusing on Central Asia and Russia.

It also claims to have provided the inspiration for the European Union Organization of Islamic Conference summit in Istanbul in 2002, in the wake of the September 11 attacks. In Turkey it has brought together leaders of the three Abrahamic religious communities, and initiated dialogues with Kurds and Alevis. Its activists and offices in Turkey have been subjected to threats and violent attacks in reaction to such endeavors.

Another method adopted by the movement as ameans of interfaith dialogue is the so-called Iftar, or fast-breaking, meals, which bring together peoples of different faiths and communities. These enable a more low-key and localized approach to interfaith and intercommunal understanding, not

Since its formation in 2007, the Intercultural Dialogue Center (Kurturler Arasi Diyalog Merkezi, KADIM) (http://www.gyv.org.tr) has functioned as a kind of clearing house for much of the movement's dialogue activity. It brings together a range of other dialogue platforms, such as the Abant Platform of the Journalists and Writers Foundations, the Intercultural Dialogue Platform, and the Dialogue Eurasia Platform.

In its various meetings, conferences, panels, publications, and other fora, these platforms seek to propagate Gulen's advocacy of tolerance and modernity, and bring together intellectuals, writers, activists, and others to discuss a wide range of current issues--some of them domestic. For example, early in 2007 Abant organized a panel in Turkey aimed at encouraging dialogue between the Sunni majority and the Alevi minority.

The Platform's first meeting was held in Abant in Turkey in 1998, but in 2004 it held its first annual meeting abroad, in Washington D.C., followed by Brussels and Paris. It was not until February 2007 that it held its first international meeting in the Islamic world, in Egypt.

Assessment

It is not possible to offer a definitive assessment of the Gulen movement's impact, either in Turkey or abroad. Its activities are too diverse both in their content and context, too devolved, and too disguised. Furthermore, the movement is a "work-in-progress," as it continues to evolve, expand, and influence. Much depends on the perspective one adopts.

Certainly in the Turkish context, the more one perceives the movement as a more-or-less hierarchical, disciplined, and "conspiratorial" organization that seeks to penetrate and undermine the Turkish state and society from within, the more one is inclined to adopt an essentially political interpretation of the movement's activities. This is precisely the model of the Gulen movement that many in Turkey's elite hold, and fear.

On the other hand, although the movement's lack of transparency and the weakness of its internal democracy and capacity for self-criticism are unsettling, this does not necessarily render it an extremist phenomenon. Neither Gulen nor the movement that takes his name is overtly politicized, and in the absence of hard evidence to the contrary, the movement will seem benign to many--unless of course one is ideologically opposed to challenges to Turkey's existing order, as many in Turkey are, or inherently uneasy about any faith-inspired movement.

A similar inconclusiveness emerges from an analysis of the movement's educational ventures. Although revenues raised by school fees are often used to enable access by less-privileged students, it remains an inescapable fact that the movement's educational model is elitist. In Turkey this is contributing to the creation of a parallel and Gulen-inspired elite.

In post-communist Central Asia, the main location of Gulen's overseas educational activities, successful applicants are usually the children either of the wealthy or of government officials. This has to be appreciated against the background of a collapsed educational, social, and economic infrastructure throughout much of the region. State spending on education has plummeted throughout the region, leading to school closures, a shortage of teachers, a degradation of the physical infrastructure, and widespread corruption surrounding school and college admissions and test results.

There is scope here for resentment of the "Turkish" schools. Although Gulen schools represent only around ten percent of Central Asia's education system, it could be that--in a tacit partnership with the Turkish state--the movement's activities will over the longer term intensify the emotive and material bonds between Turkic peoples--or their elites--and states.

The Gulen network's Central Asian elites could in time take on the forms of their Turkish counterparts, thereby encouraging the emergence of a pan-Turkic world linked by overlapping and fused identities. This could in turn ease the development of economic interactions, and even encourage closer state-to-state relationships. Such an evolution would not quite accord with the kind of "Turkish model" that Ankara's secularists have sometimes hoped might be adopted in Central Asia, but it might dovetail with the pan-Turkic aspirations of nationalist elements in Turkey.

However, there are indications that a shared Turkic ethnic and linguistic root might not be sufficient to remove all barriers to a fuller interpenetration. The movement's educational establishments in the region are frequently referred to simply as "Turkish schools," and at least initially some local inhabitants seem to have resented the speed with which Turkish institutions replaced Soviet/Russian ones after 1991.

Furthermore, there have been indications of a distasteful Turkish chauvinism and "big brother" attitude toward the Turkic peoples of Central Asia. This sense of a "foreign" and intrusive penetration has occasionally combined with a dislike of the perceived missionary self-righteousness of the movement's teachers, whose piety and dedication can grate with more secular, non-believing and frequently dispossessed Central Asians.

In addition, the autocratic secularity of the region's political leaderships, and their post-Soviet sensitivity to anything they perceive as external meddling, puts the Gulen movement's reception in the Turkic world very much at the mercy of the region's governments. During the 1990s, Uzbek President Islam Karimov cracked down on the movement's activities in his country, including a ban on the distribution of Zaman. The movement has minimal presence there today. It is unclear whether this was a reaction to the presence in his country of a religious group that he did not control, or whether it indicated retaliation against the Turkish state's harboring of Uzbek opposition leaders.

In 2005, Turkish teaching staff at the Islamic theology school at a university in Turkmenistan was sacked by the country's autocratic leader President Saparmurat Niazov. It seems that the Turkmen regime was becoming increasingly unhappy about both the pan-Turkic and Islamic ideology of the Gulen network in the country.

Beyond former Soviet Central Asia, the Taliban regime terminated the Gulen movement's activities in Afghanistan in the late 1990s owing to its disapproval both of its brand of Islam and of external interference in the country. Notwithstanding the movement's non-governmental status, incidents such as these can set back Ankara's relations with other states.

Assessments of the movement's educational activities in the non-Turkic world require a different approach. Although Gulen schools retain their elitism, receptivity to their "Turkishness"--the Turkish teachers, the Ataturk portraits, the learning of the Turkish language, and the singing of the Turkish anthem--will of course vary.

Perhaps the movement's activities in non-Turkic parts of the world might be likened to the work of the cultural agencies of the major globally- active Western powers such as the United States, the UK, and France. It is unlikely to do harm to Turkey's image and interests abroad, or to the more general cause of global understanding and tolerance. On the other hand, the relative scale of the Gulen movement's presence is so small, and Turkey's broader military, political, technological and economic footprint in such regions so light, that it is hard to see what measurable good it might do either. Yet, again, it might be wise not to rush to judgment. After all, Turkey's global profile and "soft power" is expanding, and the existence of well-educated individuals with a knowledge of and sympathy with Turkish culture might further facilitate it. Perhaps too the movement has matured to the point that "activism through good deeds" is enough.

As Gulen schools host a primarily Muslim intake and its media outlets target primarily Muslim audiences, the movement's activities feed into its global contestation over what Islam is and what role it should play. Its message could hardly be more at odds with that brand of Islam typically dubbed "fundamentalist," notwithstanding the ire of commentators such as Rubin.

Gulen's teaching might increase Muslim receptivity to the idea of a Turkish-style fusion of modernity and Islam, and might generate local bulwarks against Islamist fundamentalism. Yet it is in precisely those regions most susceptible to fundamentalist Islamism that resistance to Gulen is at its strongest. In an apparent paradox, the Gulen movement's slightest presence is in the neighboring Arab and Iranian Muslim worlds.

This is explained by its occasionally dismissive attitude towards the practice of Islam in these countries, and by its pro-Turkic and somewhat anti-Arab attitude. General Arab mistrust of Turkey in particular, external interference in general, and suspicion of alternative forms of Islam, is in any case discouraging. Shi'i Iran's refusal to permit the establishment of (Sunni) Gulen schools in its (Turkic) areas has also ensured that barriers to the Gulen message remain in place.

Even so, overtures to the Arab and Iranian worlds occur, and may be intensifying. It appears that Gulen schools can now be found in Egypt, Jordan, Yemen, and Tunisia.

The relative absence of interaction with the Arab and Iranian worlds leads to an observation about the movement's global interfaith activities too. In the present atmosphere, the movement's championing of interfaith and intercivilizational dialogue is surely welcome as an antidote to those who seem determined to prove Huntington right.

However, those engaged in interfaith dialogue are preaching largely to the converted--to each other. In a battle for hearts and minds, it is requisite to engage with precisely those variants of Islam that are disproportionately to be found in those areas of the world where the Gulen movement's footprint is at its lightest. Its venture into the Arab world, in the form of a Gulen-inspired Arabic magazine, Hira, first published in December 2005, and occasional meetings with like-minded Egyptian intellectuals, is unlikely to impress the region's radicals. On the other hand, this is a process--not an event--that produces winners and losers.

As such, it is not and may never be possible to assess definitively the impact of the Gulen movement's transnational interfaith engagement.

Gulen schools in the West have served to reinforce or preserve Turkish and Muslim identities otherwise vulnerable to dilution as a result of interaction with host societies, although the simultaneous commitment to accommodation to and tolerance of host country customs is strong.

Whether such impulses are compatible is a moot point, of course. Overall though, the emphasis placed on integration in the Gulen's Turkish minority schools in the West, and the contribution to intercommunal relations where Gulen schools serve divided communities, perhaps permit a more positive assessment of the contribution the movement makes to more localized interfaith and intercommunal dialogue and tolerance.

Conclusion

The Gulen movement eludes definition. Deeply Turkish, it is globally engaged. It is apolitical, yet constitutes an existential political threat to Turkey's officially secularist order, not least through its penetration of the state's machinery. It is opposed by the Kemalist state, yet it enhances Turkey's "soft power," its external trade, and its pan-Turkic links. It provides a challenge both to harsher forms of Islam and to those suspicious of any faith-based, and especially Islam-inspired, phenomena.

Espousing democracy and openness, it remains secretive and publicity-shy. Spiritually based, it is extremely wealthy. It is a "cult" of sorts, yet it is becoming increasingly mainstream. More a unifying set of values than an organization perhaps, its tentacles expand relentlessly nevertheless. It may over-reach itself, but it is a "work-in-progress," metamorphosing as it grows. Along with other faith-inspired political and social movements, it is changing Turkey's profile and will continue to do so. Turkey's assertively secularist elite are right to be concerned.

Gulen and CIA

In a recent immigration court case involving Turkish Islamic Leader, Fetullah Gulen, US prosecutors exposed an illegal, covert, CIA operation involving the intentional Islamization of Central Asia. This operation has been ongoing since the fall of the Soviet Union in an ongoing Cold War to control the vast energy resources of the region - Uzbekistan, Azerbaijan, Kazakhstan and Turkmenistan - estimated to be worth $3 trillion. Court Case The scene for these dramatic disclosures was an application for a Green Card in the Eastern District Court in Philadelphia by "controversial Islamic scholar" Fetullah Gulen. Gulen, who has been living in the United States since 1998, argued that he qualified for the Green Card as "an extraordinarily talented academic." The court case was covered extensively by the Turkish press. Leading Turkish newspaper Hurriyet reported:

"Gulen's financial resources were detailed in the public prosecutor's arguments, which claimed that Saudi Arabia, Iran, the Turkish government, and the Central Intelligence Agency, or CIA, were behind the Gulen movement. It stated that some businessmen in Ankara donated 10 to 70 percent of their annual income to the movement and that it corresponded to $20,000 to $300,000 per year per person. It added that one businessman in Istanbul donated $4-5 million each year and that young people graduating from Gulen's schools donated between $2,000 and $5,000 each year."

Among the reasons given by the US State Department's attorneys as to why Gulen's permanent residence application was refused, is the suspicion of CIA financing of his movement. [. . .] "There is even CIA suspicion" "Because of the large amount of money that Gulen's movement uses to finance his projects, there are claims that he has secret agreements with Saudi Arabia, Iran, and Turkic governments. There are suspicions that the CIA is a co-payer in financing these projects," claimed the attorneys. [. . .] Among the documents that the state attorneys presented, there are claims about the Gulen movement's financial structure and it was emphasized that the movement's economic power reached $25 billion. "Schools, newspapers, universities, unions, television channels . . . The relationship among these are being debated. There is no transparency in their work," claimed the attorneys."

Russian intelligence agency, the FSB, has repeatedly taken action against the Gulen movement for acting as a front organization for the CIA. In December 2002, Turkish newspaper Hurriyet reported:

"Russian secret service claims: Turkish religious brotherhood works for CIA The FSB, the Russian intelligence organization formerly called the KGB, has claimed that the 'Nurcus' religious brotherhood in Turkey has engaged in espionage on behalf of the CIA through the companies and foundations it has founded. FSB head Nikolay Patrushev has mentioned the names of these companies and foundations, saying, 'The brotherhood engages in anti-Russian activities via two companies, Serhad and Eflak, as well as foundations such as Toros, Tolerans and Ufuk.' Patrushev has accused the brotherhood of conducting pan-Turkish propaganda, of trying to convert Russian youths to Islam by sowing the seeds of enmity, and of engaging in certain lobbying activities. These companies and foundations have turned up in the internet site of Fethullah Gulen [alleged leader of the Nurcu religious community currently living in the United States who is a defendant in several court cases in Turkey, accused of engaging in anti-secularist activities.]"

Russia has banned all of Gulen's madrassas, and in April of this year, banned the Nurcu Movement completely.Gulen's Madrassas The Gulen Movement founded madrassas all over the world in the 1990's, most of them in the newly independent Turkic republics of Central Asia - Azerbaijan, Turkmenistan, Uzbekistan, Kazakhstan and Kyrgyzstan - and Russia. These madrassas appear to be used as a front for enabling CIA and State Department officials to operate undercover in the region, with many of the teachers operating under diplomatic passports.

Why Central Asia? Central Asia, with its vast energy wealth, is of major interest to US oil and gas companies. The region is also of key strategic interest in the 'Great Game' as Russia, China and the US compete for dwindling energy supplies. The US government has been using Turkey as a proxy to gain control over Central Asia via Pan-Turkic nationalism and religion. Sibel Edmonds Case Twenty six people wrote reference letters supporting Gulen's application for a Green Card - most notably ex-CIA agent George Fidas, former Turkish ambassador Morton Abramowitz, and former CIA Deputy Director Graham Fuller who appears in Sibel Edmonds' State Secrets Privilege Gallery.

Gulen Schools in USA

Turkish imam, Fethullah Gülen is known as an educator, an advocate of tolerance, and a moderate voice of Islam. Gülen's interfaith dialogue organizations are known to have opened around the globe. It is known that Gülen, the head of the neo-Nur, Gülen Movement, has inspired his followers, called the

Fethullahci, to open hundreds of educational institutions around the world. Gülen's schools in Turkey, Turkic Republics, Africa, Asia, and Europe are praised and are even the focus of academic studies. Gülen's influence and visibility on the world stage has increased dramatically in the past decade. Even with the recent surge of exposure, what is still little known or publicised about Fethullah Gülen and the Fethullahci, is that they operate one of their largest and fastest growing operations in the United States with the majority of their start-up institutions being public, charter schools.

Minnesota signed into law the first charter school legislation in the United States in 1991. Since then, 39 other states, the District of Columbia and Puerto Rico have passed charter school legislation. The majority of that legislation was signed into law between the mid 1990's and the year 2000. Gülen came to the United States in 1998 for medical treatment and, presumably, to avoid an indictment for attempting to undermine the secular, Turkish state.

Since Gülen's arrival in the U.S., there has been a substantial increase in the number of Gülen-influenced non-profit institutions formed in the United States. The growth seems to have some organization. Turkish nationals residing in the United States for employment or graduate education, will form a non-profit, interfaith dialogue organization. The stated mission of these groups is to promote education, introduce Turkish culture, promote understanding and dialogue between Americans and Turks as well as interfaith dialogue.

These organizations also sponsor dialogue trips to Turkey attended by the public as well as local state and national politicians. The education component of these groups are typically carried out by running Saturday schools or offering tutoring sessions.

Individuals directly or indirectly related to these dialogue groups will then either transition the dialogue to a "doing business as" or create a completely new non-profit educational foundation that will petition the state's Department of Education to open a charter school. Support service companies for these schools have also developed such as the Accord Institute in Southern California and Concept Schools in the Midwest. These companies offer management services and curriculum development to the associated schools.

There is also an affiliated for-profit business component. Apex Educational Services supplies many of the charter schools in the Western U.S. with information technology equipment-even sophisticated surveillance systems. Atlas Group of Ankara, Turkey owns a subsidiary in Texas named Atlas Texas Construction and Trading Inc. The company's website states, "Our company has already begun construction work of a gymnasium project named "Dove Science Academy Gymnasium" in Oklahoma, school remodeling in San Antonio and Houston."

There are also business groups that have been established such as the Texas-Turkish American Chamber of Commerce and the California Turkish American Chamber of Commerce. All of this is very similar to what Bayram Balci wrote about in his analysis of the Gülen Movement in Central Asia.

Proof that Gülen affiliated charter schools exist is difficult to find and is that way by design. Janes Islamic Affairs Analyst quotes Gülen, ""service on behalf of the movement would be discreet and quite, "and that this stance constituted the "founding philosophy of his movement."" Janes also points out that Gülen sends out mixed messages between its Turkish and English language outlets.

This is true for charter schools in the U.S. On Gülen's English website there is a Sahab article titled, "We Made Gülen's Ears Ring."

The same article can be found on Gülen's Turkish site, but there is more text than there is in the English article. The additional text on the Turkish site translates: It is estimated that the disciples of the Gülen movement have established approximately a thousand schools in 140 countries.

If 600 schools are bought this way in the United States – and that's what the members of the Gülen movement are striving to do, -and if 200 students graduate from each one of these schools, then 120 thousand sympathizers of Turkey join the mainstream out there every year. We are trying to lobby against the Armenian genocide resolution every year. And yet, through education, we can teach tens of thousands of people the Turkish language and our national anthem, introduce them to our culture and win them over. And this is what the Gülen movement is striving for.

On Gülen's website, there is a paper written by Dr. Ian G. Williams in which he states, "My way into this area of research, which has taken me in the past three years to the U.S. to visit schools related to Fethullah Gülen and to Turkey." Also, "My encouters within these schools had begun in the USA-where there are both primary/elementary and high schools." He also notes the term "Hocaefendi" "is the term with which my respondents all used when referring to Gülen and his work."

Also on Gülen's website, is a paper stating: At that point, it should be noted that, the history of the movement in Europe and in Muslim World is quite short, but as a beginning, they have a good start in the Netherlands with almost all sorts of institutions and activities, in the United States with a striking rise in the amount of state-financed charter schools and in Kurdish controlled Northern Iraq with seven schools and despite a pretty slippery ground.

A traveler on a dialogue trip to Turkey, sponsored by the Seattle, Washington Acacia Foundation wrote the following about her trip experience. "As our journey continued our primary guide discussed his experience as principal of a public charter school in Los Angeles, California that he created based upon the spiritual values of Fethullah Gülen."20 A Rabbi traveling on another dialogue trip to Turkey sponsored by the Houston, Texas Institute for Interfaith Dialog had this to say about his trip, "Of course there are many of these schools in Turkey, but also in other countries with Turkish populations, as well as in many Muslim countries such as Afghanistan and Egypt, and even in the United States. In fact, there are Gülen schools here in Houston."

Specific charter school ties to Gülen can also be established. The following is a small sampling due to the number of schools. Cosmos Foundation operates charter schools in Texas under the name Harmony Science Academy. They also have ties to established charter schools in Oklahoma and Louisiana and are petitioning the opening of a school in New Mexico.23 In a Today's Zaman article dated March 4, 2009 it reads, "We are at the Turkish Olympiads in Houston, Texas, sponsored by the Cosmos foundation, a nonprofit organization that the Fethullah Gülen movement is involved in. From their website, Niagara Education Services, Inc. in Chicago, Illinois, operates a subsidiary called

Beehive Science and Technology Academy in Salt Lake City, Utah, has been featured in the Salt Lake Tribune because of the school's alleged affiliations to Gülen. The principal of the school has said, "he supports Gülen's ideas, but wouldn't describe himself as a "follower.""

"Many of Beehive's teachers and founders also support Gülen's ideals, but he said there's no formal tie." "Some staff members personally know the Pennsylvania preacher." The principal is listed as a primary contact for the Multicultural Arch Foundation in Salt Lake City and was the Vice President of the Dialog Foundation in Reseda, California. Dialog Foundation changed its name to the Magnolia Foundation which is now doing business as Magnolia Science Academy with a number of schools in Southern California.

River City Science Academy in Jacksonville, Florida posted information about their annual Spring Break trip to Turkey. If a student's grades are high enough, twenty percent of the trip will be subsidized by the Amity Turkish Cultural Center. The third day of the trip will be spent in Istanbul with dinner at Coskun College which is noted to be a 'sister school' of FSA.

There are two issues presented here, the first being, this is River City Science Academy's trip not FSA's which is Fulton Science Academy, a charter school in Alpharetta, Georgia. Secondly, Coskun College "was founded by Fethullahci, followers of the spiritual Islamic leader Fethullah Gülen, one of the most influential people in Turkey. The pedagogical project is inspired by Gülen's principles of progress, enlightenment and development."

On the ninth day of the trip, the school visits Fatih University, a well known Gülen University. Daisy Education Corporation in Arizona operates as Sonoran Science Academy. Their Turkish Language teacher was quoted at the Turkish Language Olympics in Istanbul. The article says about those in attendance, "Nearly all the competitors are students of schools set up by a global network of millions of followers of the Turkish preacher and author."[38] Another article covering the Turkish Language and Performing Arts Contest Finals at Pacifica Institute in Irvine, California found on Gülen's website, date March 2, 2009, lists Sonoran Science Academy along with Coral Academy of Science, Bay Area Technology School, Magnolia Science Academy and Beehive Science and Technology Academy asparticipants.[39] Pacifica Institute, formerly known as, Global Cultural Connections, in December 2009,organized a Gülen Conference and is described as an organization that, "works in Southern California in support of the Gülen movement"[40] and, "the Pacifica Institute is a foundation based upon the teachingsof   Fethullah   Gülen."

The Fethullahci and others try to distance these schools and organizations from Gülen, but as the above ties show, that is not the whole truth. Even those close to the movement concede:

"In terms of formal organization, all facilities set up by Gülen's followers are independent units and promote themselves as such. Yet they are joined in an "educational network of virtue", as all the leading figures were socialized within the cemaat, participate in the cemaat's life and are connected to each other through the close interpersonal links of the cemaat."

"In the field of education, this part of the identity is however not stressed and teachers from outside the cemaat work at these schools as well. They may be non-Muslims and in many cases the pupils have never heard of Fethullah Gülen. In this sense, the schools may not be considered as Gülen-cemaat schools. But this assumption would deny the fact that without Gülen and the people of the cemaat, who view their work as a religious service, these schools would not exist.

Though these schools teach a secular curriculum in the classroom, there is still hesitancy to openly affiliate these charter schools with Gülen. Bayram Balci of the French Institute for Anatolian Studies and Hakan Yavus, professor at the University of Utah, are two of the most knowledgeable individuals as it pertains to the Gülen Movement. Balci's doctoral thesis was titled, "Fethullah Gülen's Missionary Schools in Central Asia and their Role in the Spreading of Turkism and Islam," and equates the Fethullahci's activities to that of the Jesuits.

Yavus, in an interview with Radio Free Europe and also Religioscope, says the Gülen Movement is, "a bottom-up Islamization approach of society" through education." And its goal is, "to create sympathizers around the world," "sympathizers for Gülen, sympathizers for Islam and sympathizers for Turkey." In a Reuters article Yavus states, "It is a political movement ... and it has always been political. They think power is very important. They want to train an elitist class which will then turn Turkey into a centre of the religious world, Islamise the country."

This is a potential issue forthese charter schools. The schools are funded by federal and state tax revenues. At the federal level, this means there is potential conflict with the Establishment Clause of the First Amendment of the U.S. Constitution which implies tax dollars are not allowed to fund religious institutions. The state level is where the schools could potentially have their biggest legal troubles. Most of the states' charter school legislation has language similar to that of the State of Pennsylvania which reads, "a charter school shall benon-sectarian in all operations." Some 'outsiders' have taken notice of the movement's increased activity concluding, "Gülenism is essencially a cult." and is a "cult of sorts." Coupling this all together, It is clear why these schools do not want to be labeled Gülen schools.

To date, there are around 120 of these affiliated charter schools in the United States. Many of these schools are academically successful, producing above average student assessment scores. State's have labeled some of the schools as "exemplary"50 and US News and World Report ranks some of the schools as the "Best High Schools in the Country."51 Many parents seem happy with the education their students are receiving. Partly due to the school's success and more to do with the fervor of the Fethullahci, there has been a tremendous surge in the opening of these schools over the past five years. This momentum does not seem to be slowing, even with numerous states cutting education budgets due to poor economic conditions. Next Fall, at least another half dozen schools across the country will be opening their doors.

With rapid growth and increased, nationwide visibility, it is inevitable that more scrutiny and questions will be raised as to the nature of these schools. It will be interesting to watch how the Movement and the schools respond to   this   attention   in   the   future.

The End game

Milli Gorus VS Hizmet Cemaati

The core of the AKP comes from the "National View" (Milli Gorus) tradition, which can be best defined as Turkey's version of political Islam with anti-Western and pan-Islamic tones. Although the AKP explicitly abandoned this ideology during its founding more than a decade ago, most observers think Erdogan is gradually reverting back to the "National View" in the past few years.

The Gulen movement, however, comes from the tradition of Islamic scholar Said Nursi (1878-1960), who focused on faith and morality rather than politics, and whose followers generally shied away from political Islam. Hence, Gulen's followers never voted for Milli Gorus and opted for center-right parties. Some scholars have thus defined the Gulen movement as "cultural Islam" as opposed to political Islam.

Had the Gulen movement been limited only to cultural Islam, this current tension would be limited. Most observers agree that the movement in fact has its own version of a political effort: aiming for members to obtain jobs within the judiciary and the police. Apparently, this began back in the '70s as an effort to transform a hostile state — Turkey's draconian secular regime — by gradually joining its ranks. Since it has been a covert task, it has always been a matter of speculation and a source for conspiracy theories.

When the AKP came to power in 2002 and soon found itself targeted by the old secular guard, the Gulen followers within the police and the judiciary emerged as a natural ally. Thus Erdogan, it is often said, empowered these fellow conservatives against their secularist rivals. However, once the old establishment was decisively defeated, sometime around 2010 to 2011, disagreements emerged between the AKP and the Gulen movement.

MIT Crisis

The first breaking point was the so-called "MIT (Turkish National Intelligence Organization) crisis." In February 2012, MIT head Hakan Fidan, a confidant of Erdogan, was called by an Istanbul prosecutor to testify as part of an investigation into the Kurdistan Workers Party (PKK).

This was, as *The New York Times* then reported, *"the latest round in a power struggle between the country's security forces and its intelligence agency."* It was also widely interpreted as a power struggle between pro-Gulen police/judiciary and the AKP. Since then, Erdogan's supporters complain of a "parallel state" within the state, which allegedly acts according its own internal hierarchy and uses state power for its own purposes.

Since the "MIT crisis" of February 2012, the AKP-Gulen movement relations have been silently sour. But in mid-November 2013, all hell broke lose when Erdogan planned to close down "prep schools," or weekend courses that prepare high school students for university exams. Since about a quarter of these schools are operated by the Gulen movement, and are a source of both finance and recruitment, the movement perceived this move as an attack. The pro-Gulen media opposed the government's "attack on private enterprise." The government responded with harsh statements, and the war of words was soon declared an "open war."

This battle between *"an increasingly authoritarian political leadership and its ever more nervous rival,"* as described by Al-Monitor columnist Yasemin Congar, took a new turn on Dec. 16, when Hakan Sukur, a football star turned parliamentarian, resigned from the AKP. Sukur, who heavily criticized the government upon resignation, is a proud follower of Gulen, and his entry into the parliament in 2011 was seen as a sign of a marriage between the movement and the party. His resignation signaled a divorce.

The government dismantled the Gulen community's cadres in the police intelligence services, shifting officers known as Gulenists to passive positions.

The special-authority courts, believed to be dominated by Gulenist judges and prosecutors, were abolished, with the amendment taking effect once the courts wrapped up the cases they were handling.

The government shielded MIT chief Fidan against the judiciary through legal amendments. It is no longer possible for prosecutors to take any action against Fidan without the prime minister's permission.

The prep schools

The spark that fueled the war was a scoop that the Zaman daily, the flagship of the Gulenist media, published coverage on Nov. 13 about a draft law indicating that the AKP is readying to close down the prep schools in the 2013-14 school year.

University and secondary school admissions in Turkey are determined through nationwide centralized exams, since the total number of students hugely outnumbers school capacity. The fierce competition has been coupled with a chronic quality deficit at public schools. Thus, the establishment and growth of private schools preparing students for the exams has become inevitable.

The Hizmet (Service) movement — or the Gulen community, as it is widely known in Turkey — owes its domestic clout mainly to the thousands of prep and regular schools it began to open in the 1970s. Since then, it has grown into a global sociopolitical Islamic movement thanks significantly to the schools it also opened around the world.

Closing the prep schools by law would no doubt deal a major blow to the community. There is also a social aspect to the issue, given that the prep schools employ about 100,000 people.

According to Zaman, the prep schools will have to be converted to regular high schools or face closure, if the draft law is passed in its current form. The daily says only 263 of the existing 3,100 prep schools could transform themselves to high schools, which means that the overwhelming majority would have to close. Those which do not comply with the law would face heavy fines of at least 500,000 Turkish lira ($250,000).

The Sabah daily, known to be close to the AKP, responded to Zaman on Nov. 15 with a front-page story, titled "Black propaganda about prep schools." The education minister branded the Zaman report "a campaign of obvious lies and provocation."

The same day, Zaman appeared with a front-page headline that declared the law to be "unprecedented even in military coup eras." Later in the day, an audio recording of the community's spiritual leader, Fethullah Gulen, was released on the hergul.org web site, which routinely carries his talks. Gulen, too, likened the closure plan to the oppression of military coup eras. "We've been through that since the 1960 coup; we've been slapped in the face. We've been through the 1970 coup and got kicked. We've been through the 1980 coup and got kicked again. But the scores are now being settled with those who slapped and kicked us," he said.

Gulen was widely thought to be likening the government to a "pharaoh" in his ensuing remarks. "If people concerned with mundane interests in every realm are against you, if the Pharaoh is against you, if Croesus is against you, then you are walking on the right path. ... It's very important to clench your teeth when calamities are coming down on you like a sledgehammer," he said. The community, meanwhile, is waging an extensive social media campaign against the closing of the prep schools.

It should be noted that the prep schools are not a matter of public debate in Turkey. The people have no negative perception of or complaints against those institutions. Thus, it is not possible to argue that the government's plan to shut the schools is a move to meet a popular demand. So, the only other argument is that the government's motivation is to punish the Gulen community.

Government ministers have so far reacted in a low-key manner to the community's indignation. In a TV interview on Nov. 14, Education Minister Nabi Avci denied they were working on a draft law like the one reported by Zaman, saying that the objective was to gradually transform the prep schools into high schools. Deputy Prime Minister Bekir Bozdag, for his part, said the issue was not a hastily decided step but has been on the government's agenda for three years.

The Corruption probe

The investigations made public on Dec. 17, 2013 revealed the biggest corruption and bribery scandal in the history of the republic, in which some members of the Justice and Development Party (AK Party) government as well as family members of President Recep Tayyip Erdoğan were allegedly implicated.

The investigations were, however, stalled by the president and prominent figures in the government. Since the investigations were made public in December 2013, Erdoğan has sought to discredit the prosecutors and policemen behind the investigations by accusing them of working to oust the AK Party from power. The prosecutors and policemen -- along with tens of thousands of others -- have already been displaced.

The investigations are known as efforts by the judiciary and the police force to fight a corruption ring made up of ministers, bureaucrats and businessmen. The amounts of money involved in the alleged activities of the corruption ring register in the ballpark of billions of dollars. The investigations into corruption, tender-rigging, unlawful gains and bribery allegations began in March 2012. They were led by prosecutors Celal Kara and Muammar Akkaş. Both were eventually removed from the cases.

The alleged crimes -- as mentioned by the prosecutors -- include: *"The transfer of lands with a value of billions of dollars at very low prices, seizure of mines from businessmen by force, tender-rigging, illegally giving state tenders worth billions of dollars to businessmen, changing the status of protected areas through bribery, opening these up to construction and making giant profits off of them."*

It all started on Dec. 17, 2013. Turkey was shaken by early morning police raids that resulted in the detention of the sons of three now-former ministers, a state bank manager, a mayor and high-profile businessmen with close ties to the government. Among the businessmen was Reza Zarrab, an Iranian living in Turkey. Some of the suspects were arrested -- albeit briefly -- after the operation.

Zarrab was accused of managing a network used to launder at least 87 billion euros to circumvent international sanctions against Iran. In addition, he allegedly bribed ministers, their sons and public officials to keep his network working. According to prosecutors' findings, Zarrab distributed TL 139 million in bribes. Around TL 11 million of this sum allegedly went to former Economy Minister Zafer Çağlayan's son, Salih Kaan Çağlayan. The investigation details also revealed that former Interior Minister Muammer Güler received a $5 million bribe from Zarrab in exchange for granting Turkish citizenship to the Iranian businessman on exceptional grounds. Furthermore, Minister Çağlayan was accused of accepting a valuable watch worth 300,000 Swiss francs (TL 700,000) as a bribe from Zarrab.

In addition, police found $4.5 million in cash stuffed into shoeboxes and about TL 10 million also in cash in a bookshelf in now-former Halkbank General Manager Süleyman Arslan's house. Zarrab allegedly sent 500,000 euros in bribes to former EU Affairs Minister Egemen Bağış. In addition, former Environment and Urban Planning Minister Erdoğan Bayraktar was accused of paving the way for building contractors to obtain illegal profits.

On Dec. 25, three ministers resigned from their posts while one other was removed from the Cabinet. Bayraktar publicly said that Erdoğan, who was prime minister at the time, should also quit, as most of the amendments to construction plans in environmentally protected zones mentioned in the corruption investigation were made on Erdoğan's orders.

Also on Dec. 25, 2013 the İstanbul Chief Public Prosecutor's Office ordered the detention of 30 suspects. Around $100 billion in bribes were said to be involved in the case. Among the main suspects of the investigation was Erdoğan's son, Bilal, businessmen Mehmet Cengiz and Latif Topbaş and

Yasin al-Qadi, a Saudi Arabian businessman who is on the US Treasury Department's "Specially Designated Global Terrorist" list.

The İstanbul Police Department, which saw an extensive purge of its top officers following the Dec. 17 corruption operation, did not comply with the order, however. Shortly after the order, prosecutors involved in the Dec. 25 investigation were removed from office on the grounds that they had abused their authority. The government assigned new prosecutors to the investigation in an apparent move to drop charges against corruption suspects.

Bilal Erdoğan was accused of receiving unlawful donations at the Foundation of Youth and Education in Turkey (TÜRGEV), on whose executive board he sits. TÜRGEV is at the center of the corruption investigation, which includes serious allegations of bribery and irregularities within the foundation. Prosecutors involved in the probe claimed that Bilal Erdoğan abused his father's influence to help TÜRGEV purchase valuable land in several provinces at prices far below market value. Various news reports have emerged over the past few months detailing the how certain plots of land and recreational facilities have been donated to TÜRGEV by certain municipalities.

Since Dec. 17,2013 Erdoğan has claimed the corruption investigations were a coup attempt by influential international groups and their proxies in Turkey to topple the AK Party government. He praised Zarrab for his contribution to the country's economy and charity events.

In addition, he targeted the "parallel structure," a clear reference to sympathizers of the faith-based Hizmet movement inspired by Turkish Islamic scholar Fethullah Gülen. He said the corruption probes were orchestrated by the movement to oust the government.

He declared a "war" against Hizmet and ordered the arbitrary reassignment of bureaucrats, members of the judiciary and the police force, who he believes are followers of the Hizmet movement. The number of reassigned officials now exceeds 40,000. The fact that no internal investigation had been launched before those officials were reassigned and that most of them were not given any explanation for their reassignment has led to comments that the government -- per Erdoğan's orders -- is carrying out a witch hunt against its critics.

Erdoğan virtually confessed to carrying out a witch hunt in a public address in May. When commenting on the reassignments, he -- without providing any evidence whatsoever -- accused the reassigned officers of "betraying Turkey" for their suspected links to the faith-based Hizmet movement, which he currently views as "enemy number one."

"If reassigning individuals who betray this country is called a witch hunt, then, yes, we will carry out a witch hunt," Erdoğan said. However, he has yet to give a satisfactory explanation about a number of leaked documents and voice recordings that suggest he, his family members and some government officials have engaged in unlawful activities.

In one of the recordings, Erdoğan and his son Bilal are allegedly heard talking about a plan how to get rid of huge sums of money stashed at several houses during the Dec. 17 corruption operation. Erdoğan, at the beginning of the recorded conversations, briefs Bilal about the operation and asks him to "zero" the money by distributing it among several businessmen. Towards the end of the conversations, Bilal tells his father that he and others have "finished the tasks you gave us," implying that the whole sum was "zeroed."

Erdoğan dismissed the authenticity of the recordings, saying they were doctored. However, official documents by the National Police Department suggest that the recordings are authentic. In another recorded conversation, Erdoğan was allegedly heard accepting two villas from businessman Mustafa Latif Topbaş in return for easing zoning restrictions in İzmir's Urla district.

Last but not least, Erdoğan is accused of helping Yasin al-Qadi, a Saudi businessman listed as a terror financier by international organizations, enter Turkey several times even though al-Qadi had been banned by the Cabinet from entering the country.

Former İstanbul Police Department financial crimes unit head Yakup Saygılı, who was placed under arrest on Thursday after being detained for carrying out the Dec. 17 and 25 operations, said during his testimony to the police that al-Qadi entered Turkey several times thanks to Erdoğan's security guards when Erdoğan was prime minister. According to Saygılı, al-Qadi could not have entered Turkey without the help and influence of Erdoğan. In addition, Saygılı said, al-Qadi was provided with a false passport to enter Turkey and a villa to use during his stay in the country.

Iran and Israel

At the heart of the corruption scandal is Turkey's gold-for-oil trade with Iran. According to the claims, Turkey made this deal in order to bypass US-EU sanctions on Iran, and Turkish state-owned Halkbank acted as the main agent of the money transfer.

No wonder one of the suspects in custody is Suleyman Aslan, CEO of Halkbank, in whose home millions of dollars were allegedly found in the now-famous shoeboxes. Another prominent suspect is Riza Sarraf, a wealthy Iranian businessman who deals with gold and was originally named Reza Zarrab. He is accused of having given bribes to prominent politicians.

In response, the pro-AKP media imply that the covert trade with Iran was merely for Turkish national interests, and the money in personal homes would be used for charitable purposes such as building schools. Moreover, according to the same media, the real culprit behind this "coup" effort is Israel. The reasoning is that the biggest enemy of Iran, and Iranian-Turkish ties, is Israel and its US lobby, so these powers must be behind the corruption probe.

The fact that the Gulen movement has carefully avoided joining the anti-Israeli sentiment within Turkey's Islamic circles (including Gulen's much discussed opposition to the Gaza Flotilla of 2010) is taken as evidence for the Israeli conspiracy. Pro-AKP media are full of articles these days that depict the Gulen movement as the fifth column or the Trojan Horse of "Zionism."

The liberals

Many liberals had tired with the AKP long before, or at least during, the Gezi Park protests of last summer. So, most of these liberals support the corruption probe, and thus appear to be in a political alliance with the Gulen movement. There are other liberals, however, who still support the AKP based on the importance they attach to the peace process between the government and the PKK. This second group of liberals is also quite suspicious about the "parallel state" — a euphemism for the Gulen movement in the judiciary and police — and warns about its hawkish and "anti-peace" stance with regard to the PKK.

Meanwhile, most other Islamic groups (none of them as big and prominent as the Gulen movement) are united behind Erdogan. Secularists are in shock and are weeping for what happened to the secular republic at the hands of two opposing Islamic cliques.

Arrest Warrant

The lawyer for Turkish Islamic scholar Fethullah Gülen, Nurullah Albayrak, in reaction to Turkish media reports on Tuesday of another arrest warrant being issued for his client, said in a statement that according to the law on criminal procedure, it is unlawful for a court to issue an arrest warrant unless the accused has been appropriately called to appear before the court. In what would seem to be another unjustified, government-motivated judicial action against the Gülen movement, a civil society organization inspired by Gülen's views, the İstanbul 3rd Penal Court of Peace issued an arrest warrant on Tuesday for Gülen, and for journalist Emre Uslu, at İstanbul Deputy Chief Public Prosecutor İrfan Fidan's request, the Hürriyet daily website reported on Tuesday.

Albayrak noted that Gülen, who has resided in the US since 1999 and whose address is public knowledge, must be summoned by Turkish and the US authorities for testimony, according to legal agreements between the two countries, before an arrest warrant can be issued. Albayrak also underlined that according to Article 98 of the Code on Criminal Procedure (CMK, Law 5271), a court can only issue an arrest warrant if the accused has not responded to an order to appear that is appropriately delivered to his current address.

Rejecting Fidan's accusations, Albayrak stated that the warrant is unacceptable according to the principles of international law and to the conscience of the people to accuse Gülen without concrete evidence showing that he is involved in a crime. According to the Turkish anti-terror law, no individual or group united under an ideology can be accused of terrorism-related crimes unless they are involved in violence.

According to the story on the Hürriyet daily website, in his letter to the İstanbul 3rd Penal Court of Peace, Fidan accused Gülen and Uslu of being involved in the establishment and administration of an armed terror organization, an attempt to overthrow the government of the Turkish Republic and acquiring top secret state documents through espionage.

Albayrak said in his statement that the court decision shows that the judiciary is being used as a tool to suppress people and groups who do not share the same views as the ruling government. "When this dark period has ended, we believe that these unlawful practices will be tried in accordance with the Constitution and the people's conscience," Albayrak said.

In December 2014, as part of a government-orchestrated operation against the media affiliated with the Gülen movement, the İstanbul 1st Penal Court of Peace issued an arrest warrant for Gülen and requested that the scholar be extradited from the United States, which is seen as a step toward the request of for an Interpol Red Notice, and ultimately extradition from the US. However, US law requires that the crime be recognized in both countries' jurisdictions and that the offense not be political in nature.

The ruling Justice and Development party (AK Party) government has asked for the extradition of Gülen from the US several times since two major graft operations incriminating the inner circle of then-Prime Minister Recep Tayyip Erdoğan and his family went public on Dec. 17 and 25, 2013. The government received negative replies from the authorities in America, due to a lack of evidence to support the charges. President Recep Tayyip Erdoğan also personally asked US President Barack Obama to "deport" Gülen several times since the graft probe.

The winner

The Gulen movement is not a political party, and there is no other political party that it will be totally comfortable with. That is why some speculate that the movement is not anti-AKP but merely anti-Erdogan, and that it hopes for a post-Erdogan and less assertive AKP.

Whoever wins, the victory can only be Pyrrhic. If Erdogan crushes the Gulen movement by any means, as some speculate these days, he will lose many votes and further diminish his democratic credentials. If the Gulen movement wins, it will only be proclaiming that it has a lot of power within the state, which will harm its reputation of being a moderate expression of "cultural Islam." Meanwhile, Turkey's political and economic stability will suffer, not to mention its rule of law and societal peace.

www.ingramcontent.com/pod-product-compliance
Lightning Source LLC
Chambersburg PA
CBHW081001290526
45795CB00009B/3037